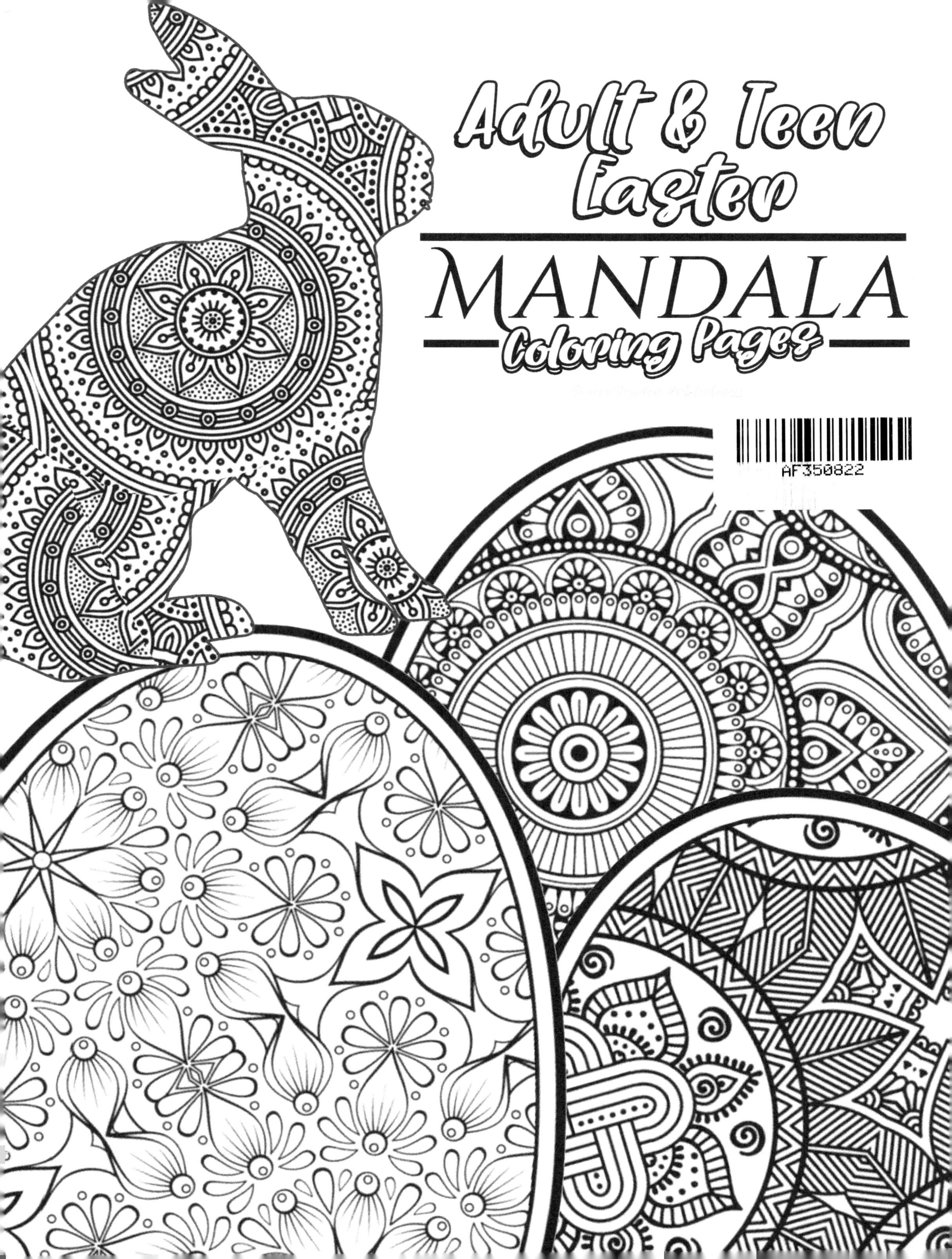

Adult & Teen
Easter
MANDALA
Coloring Pages
AF350822

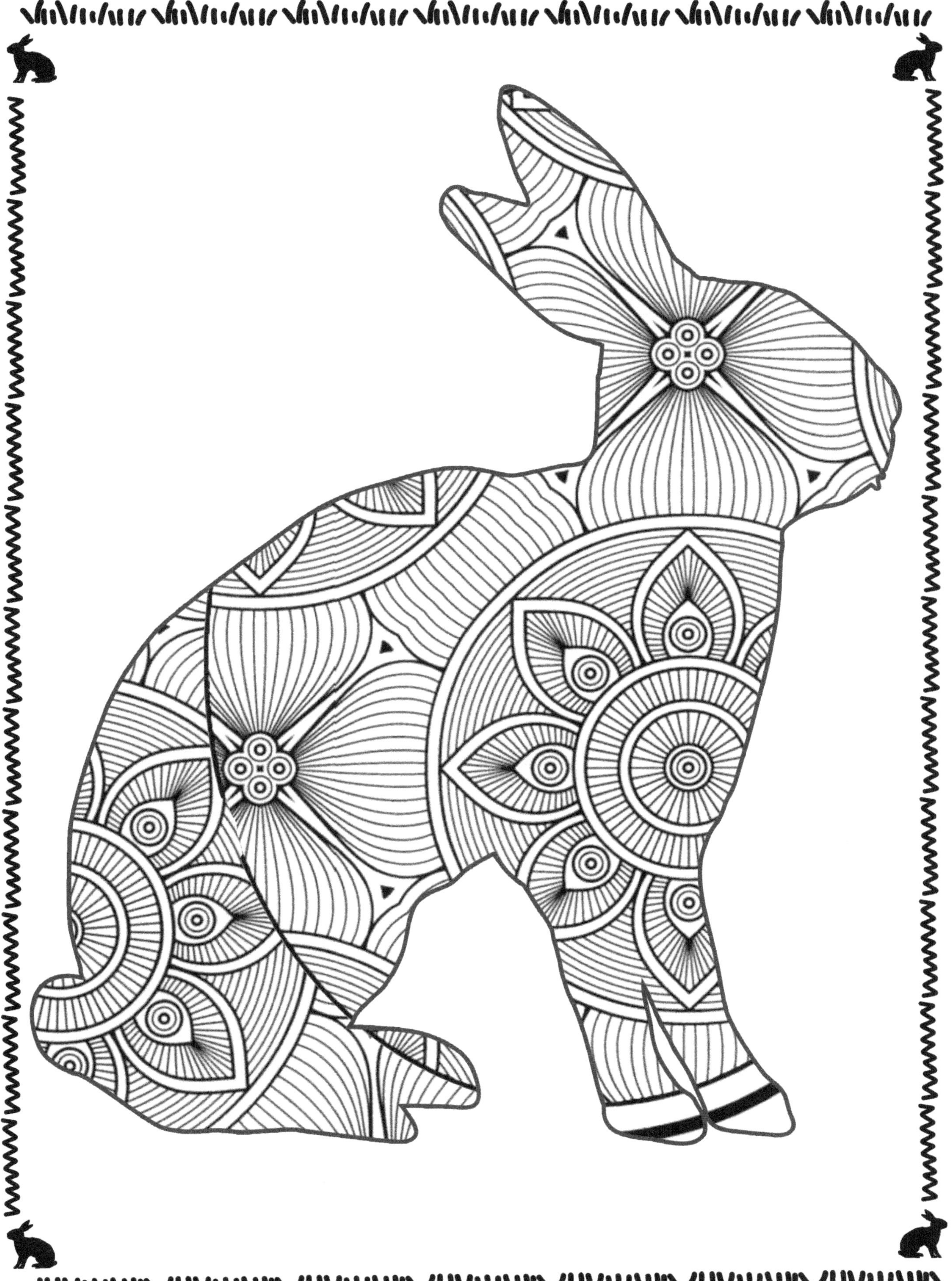

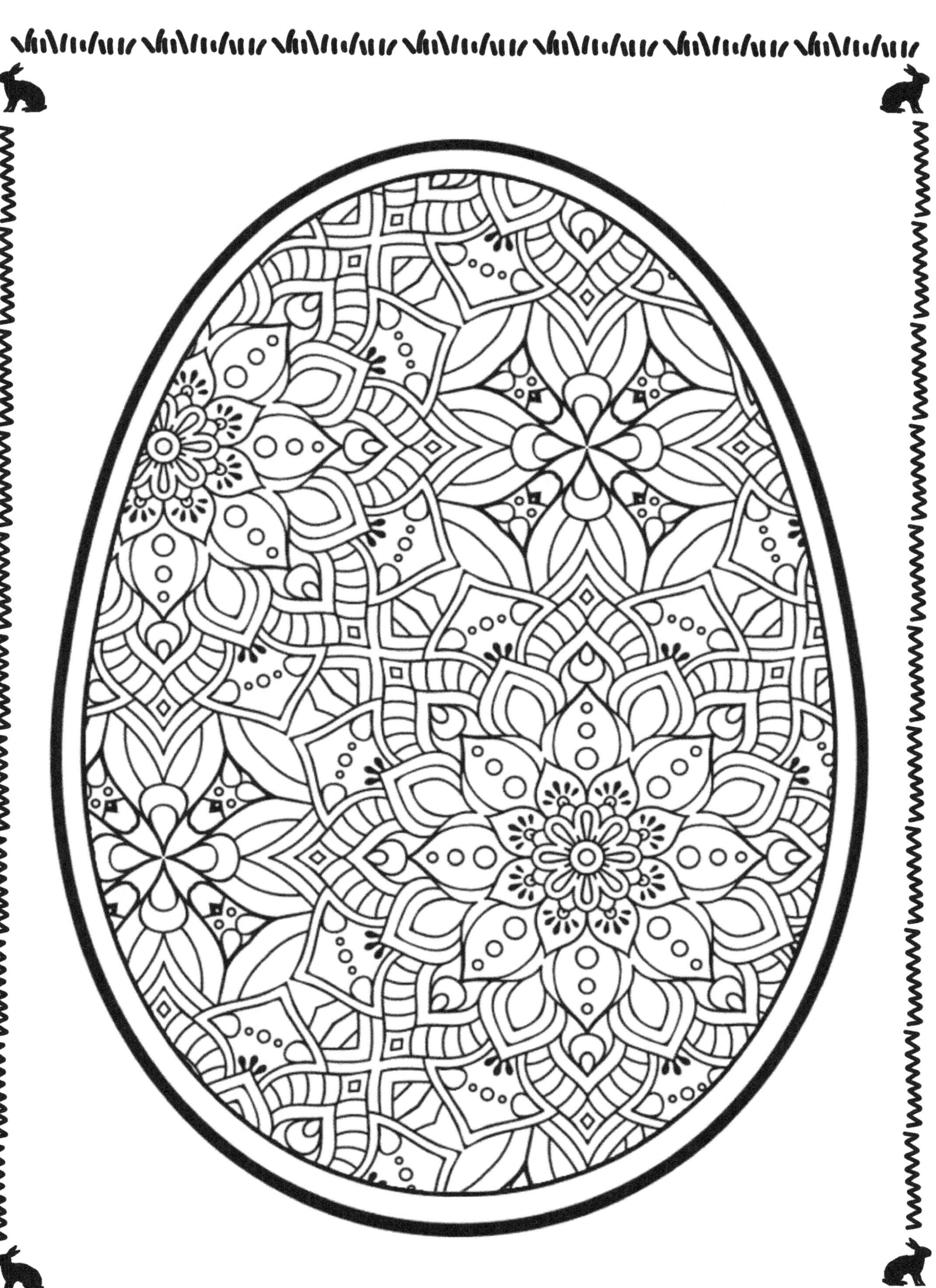

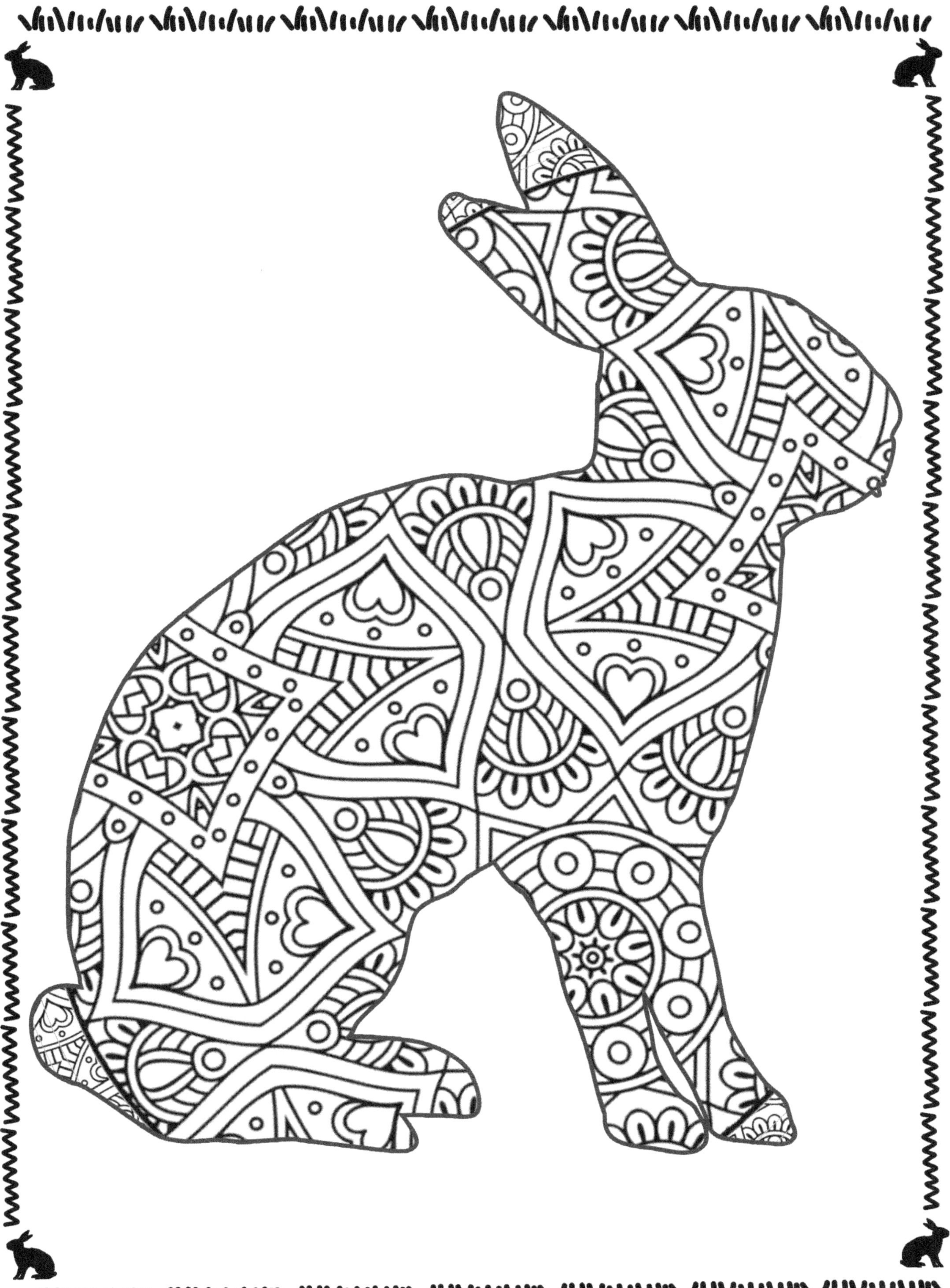

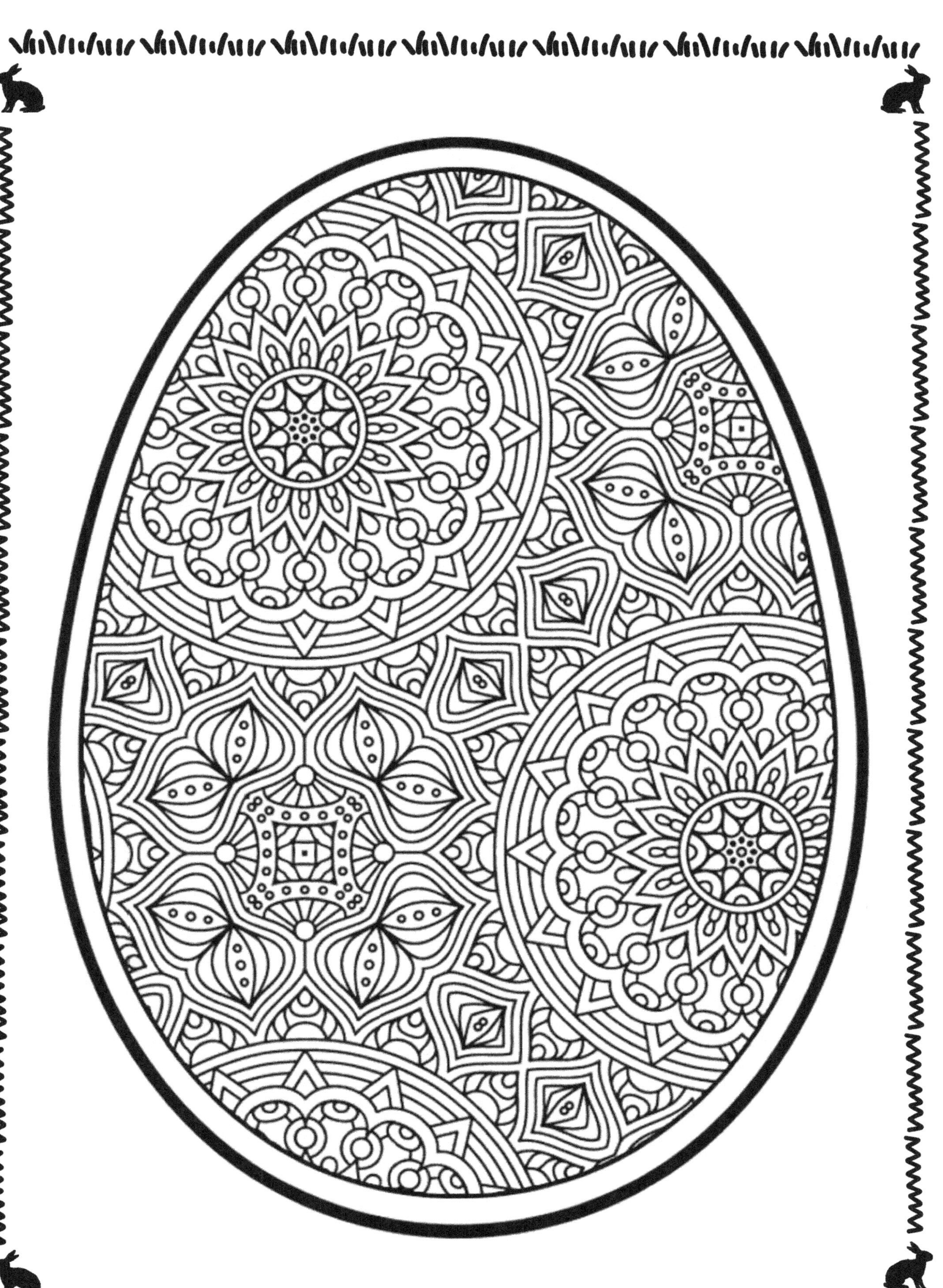

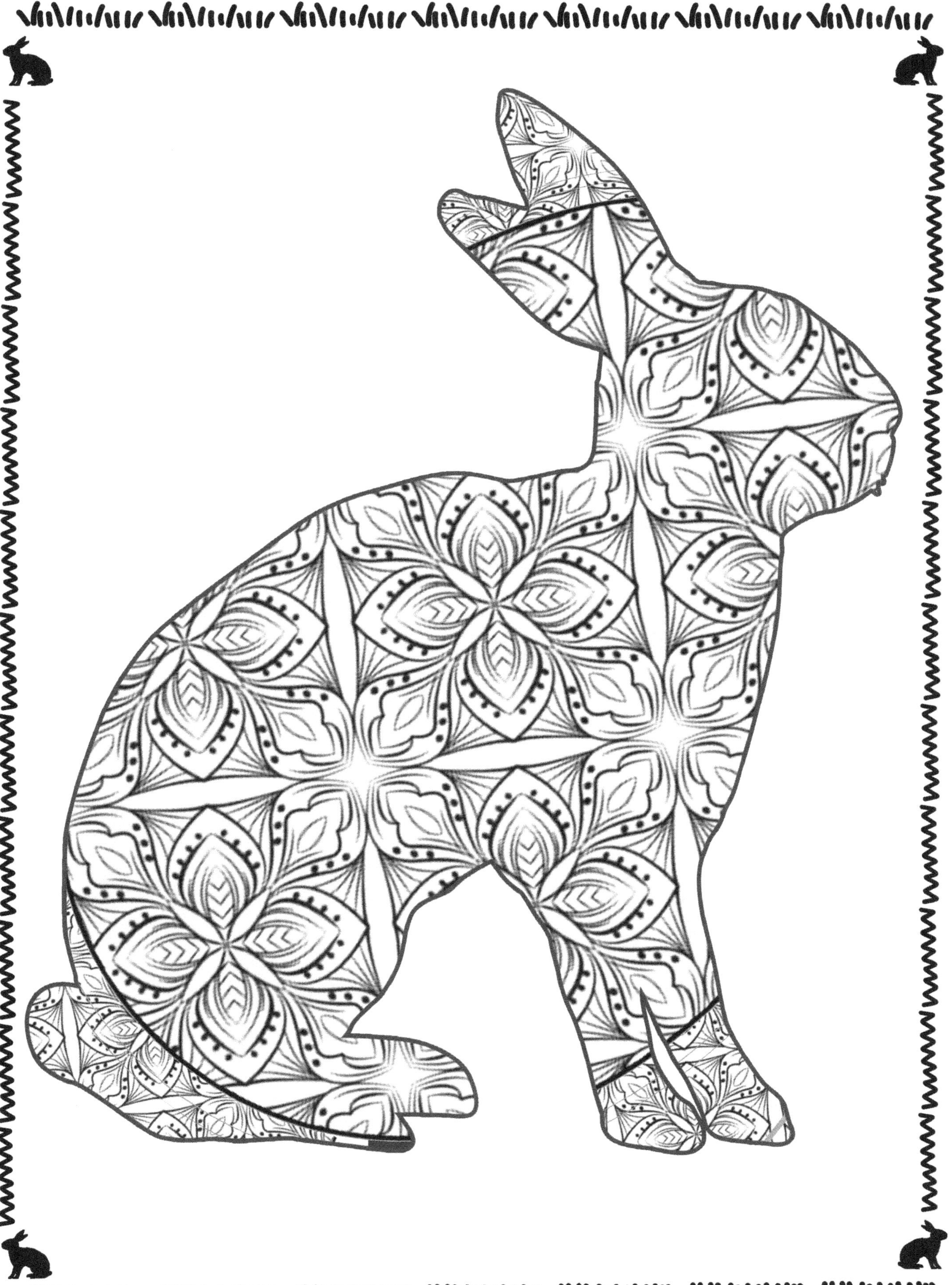

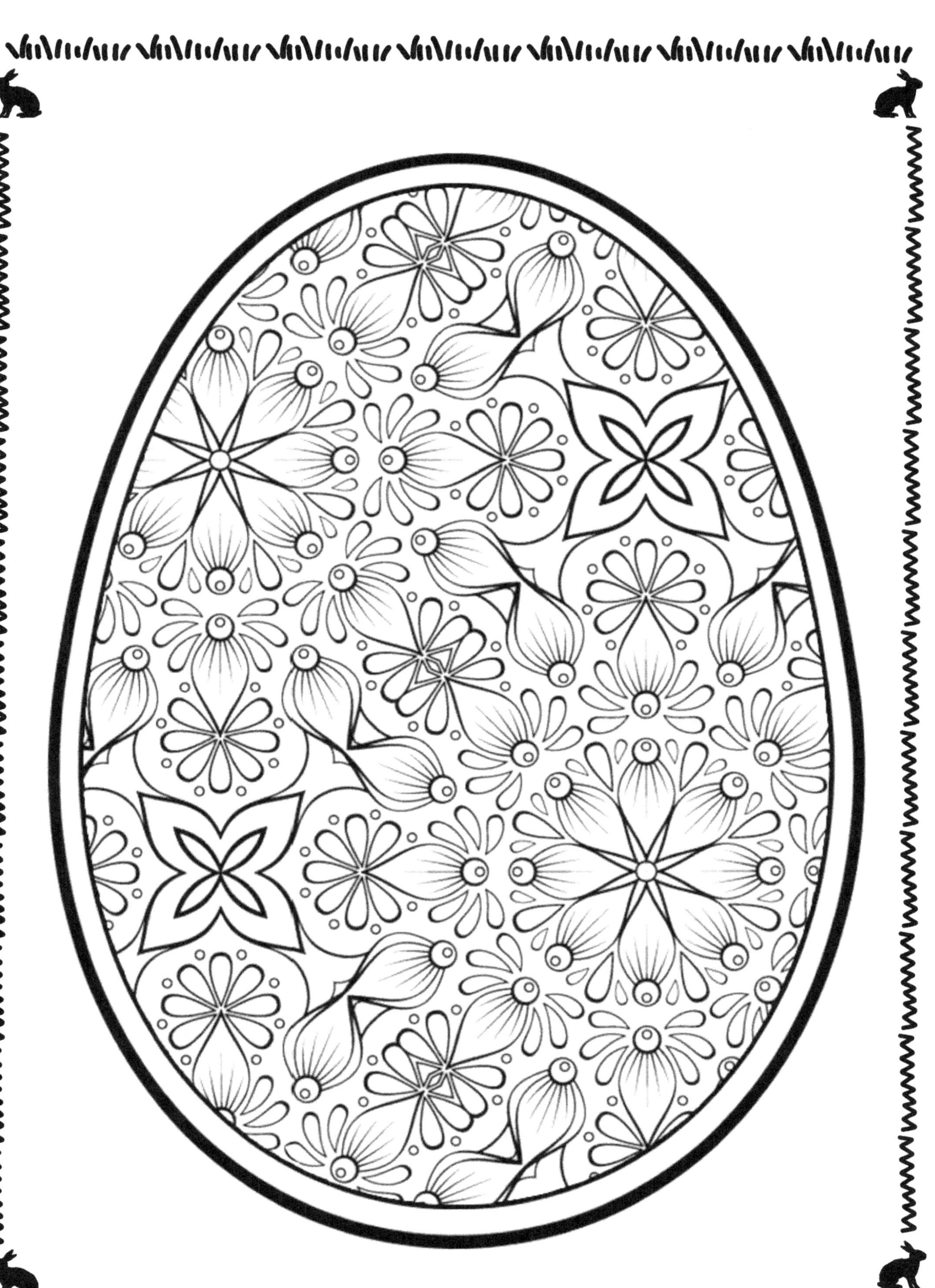

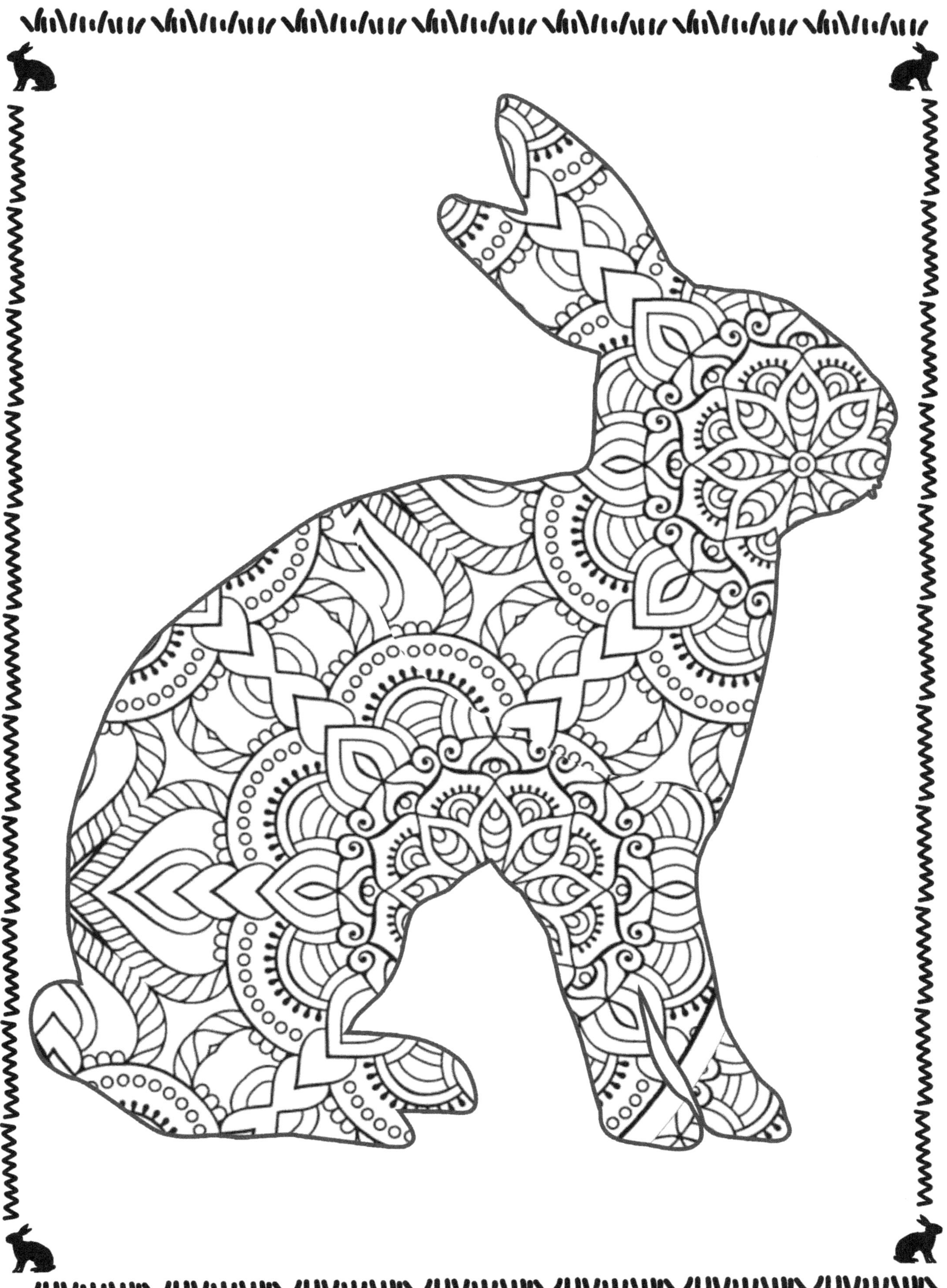

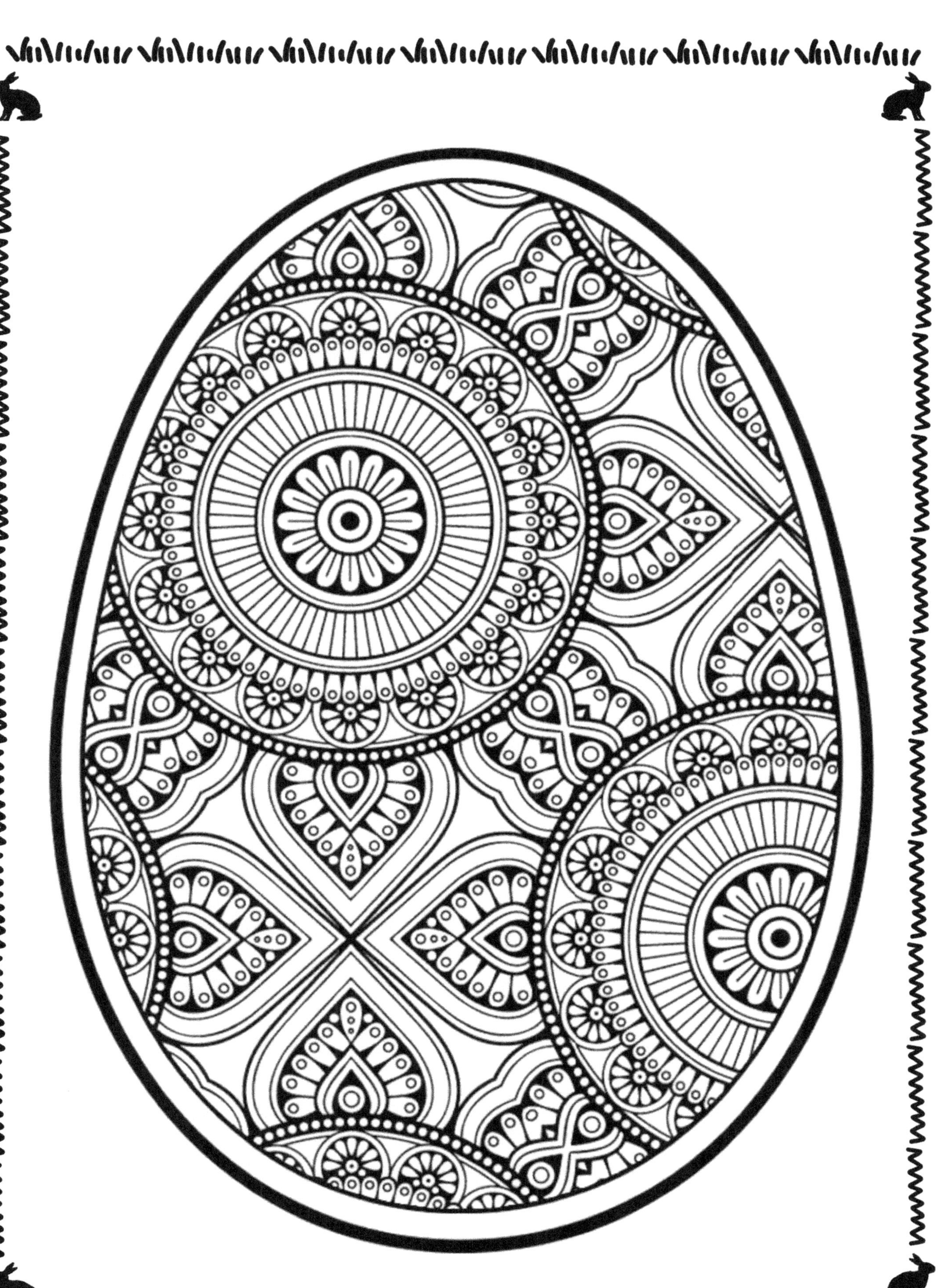

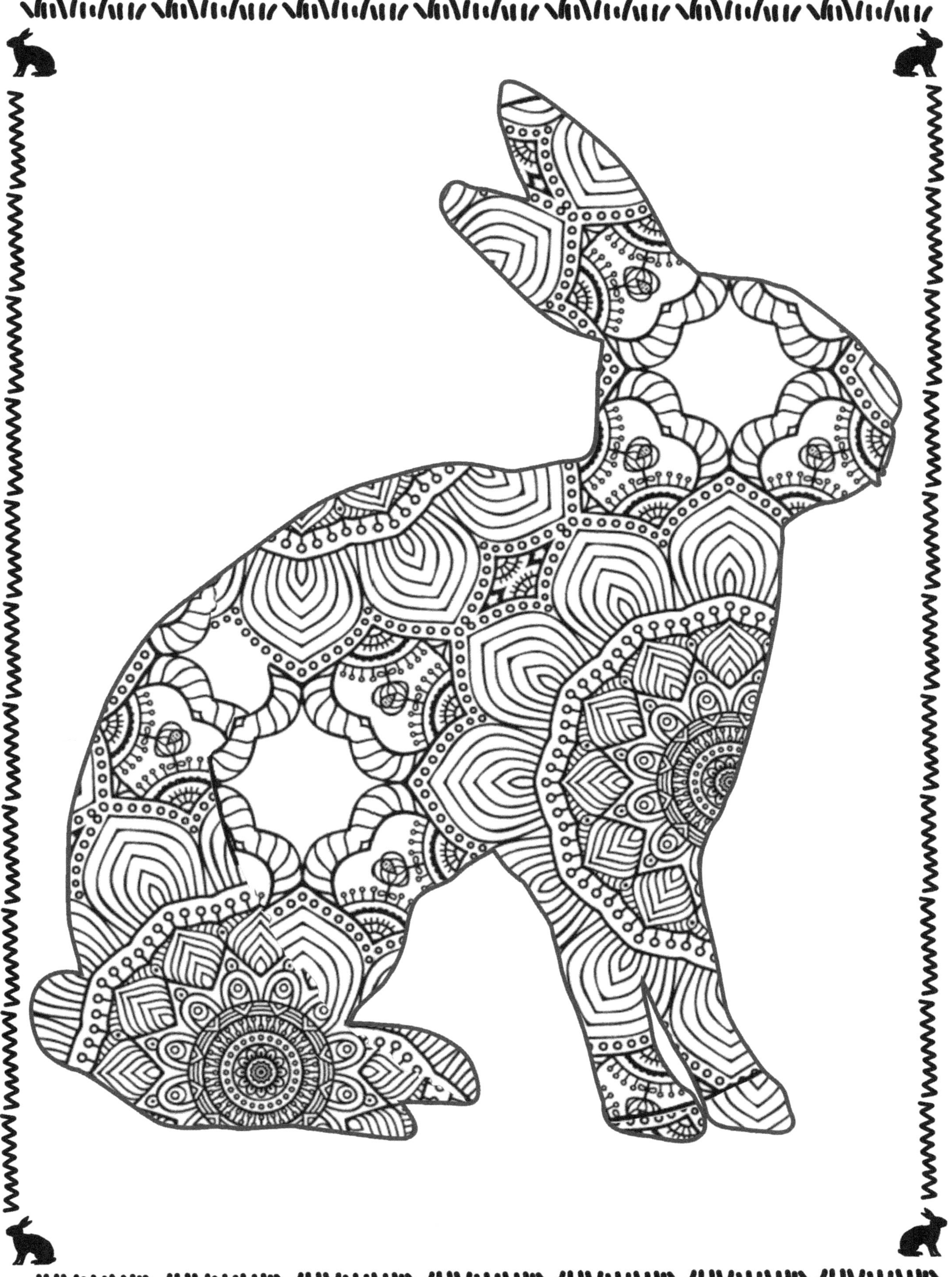

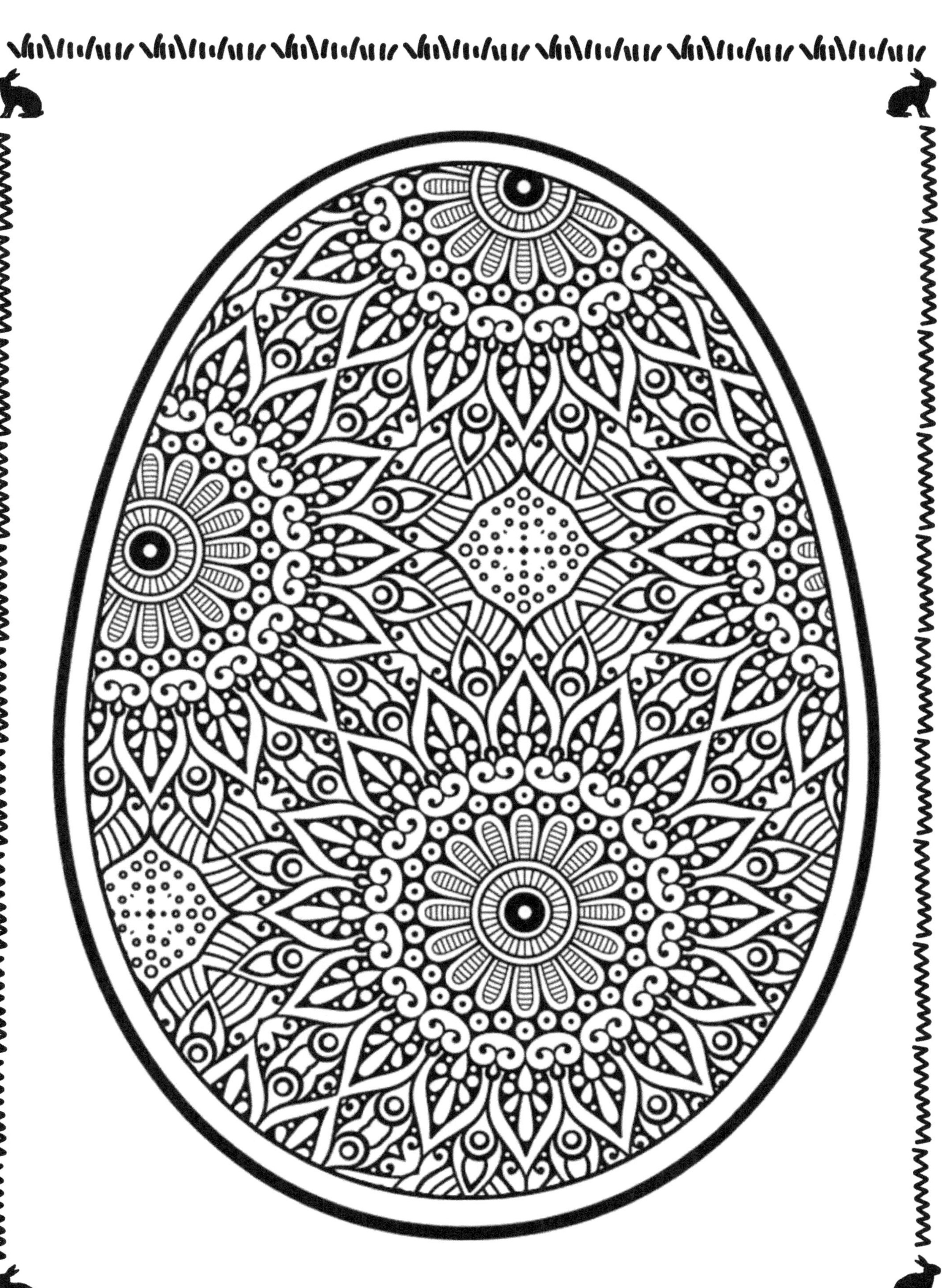

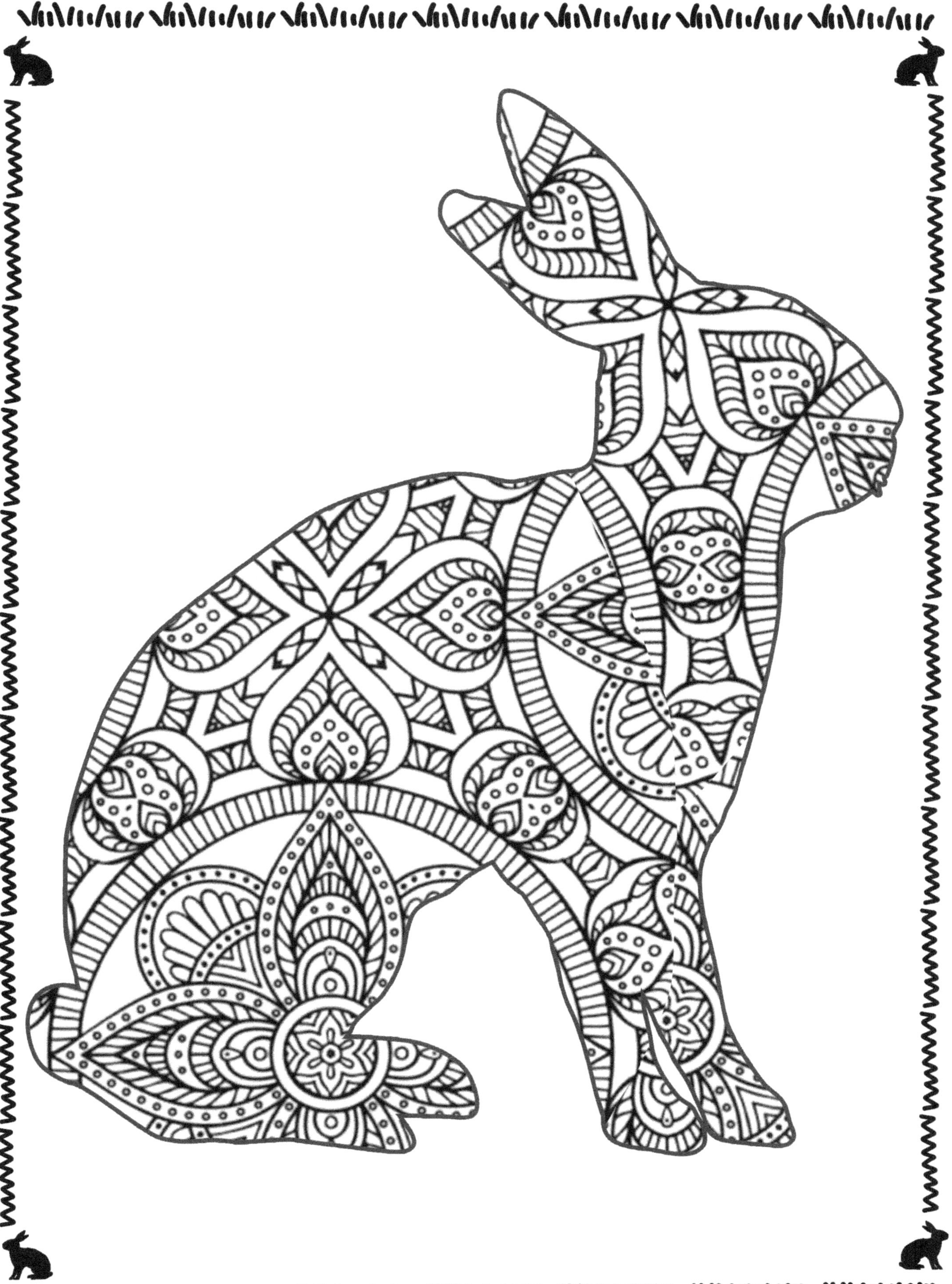

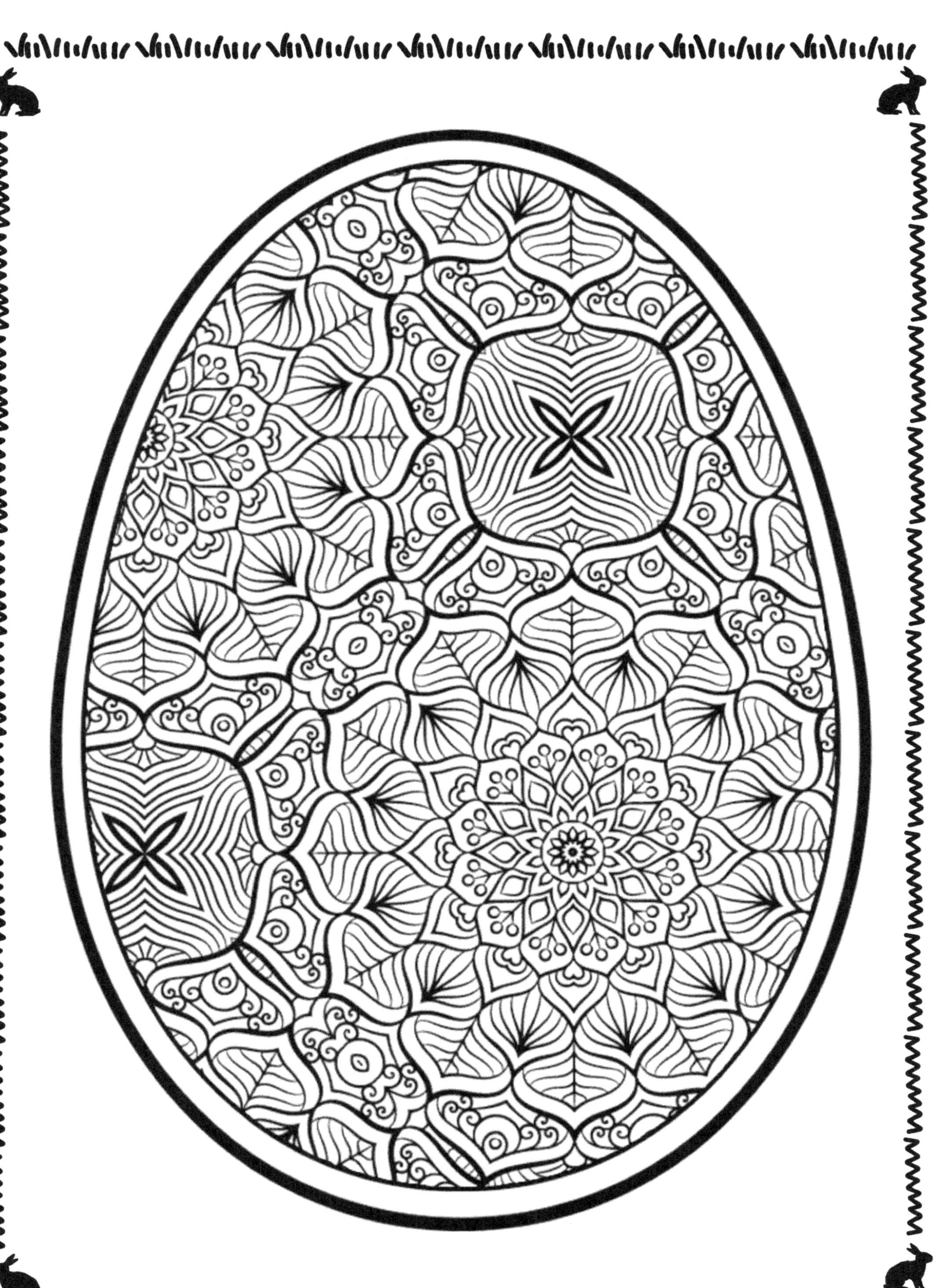

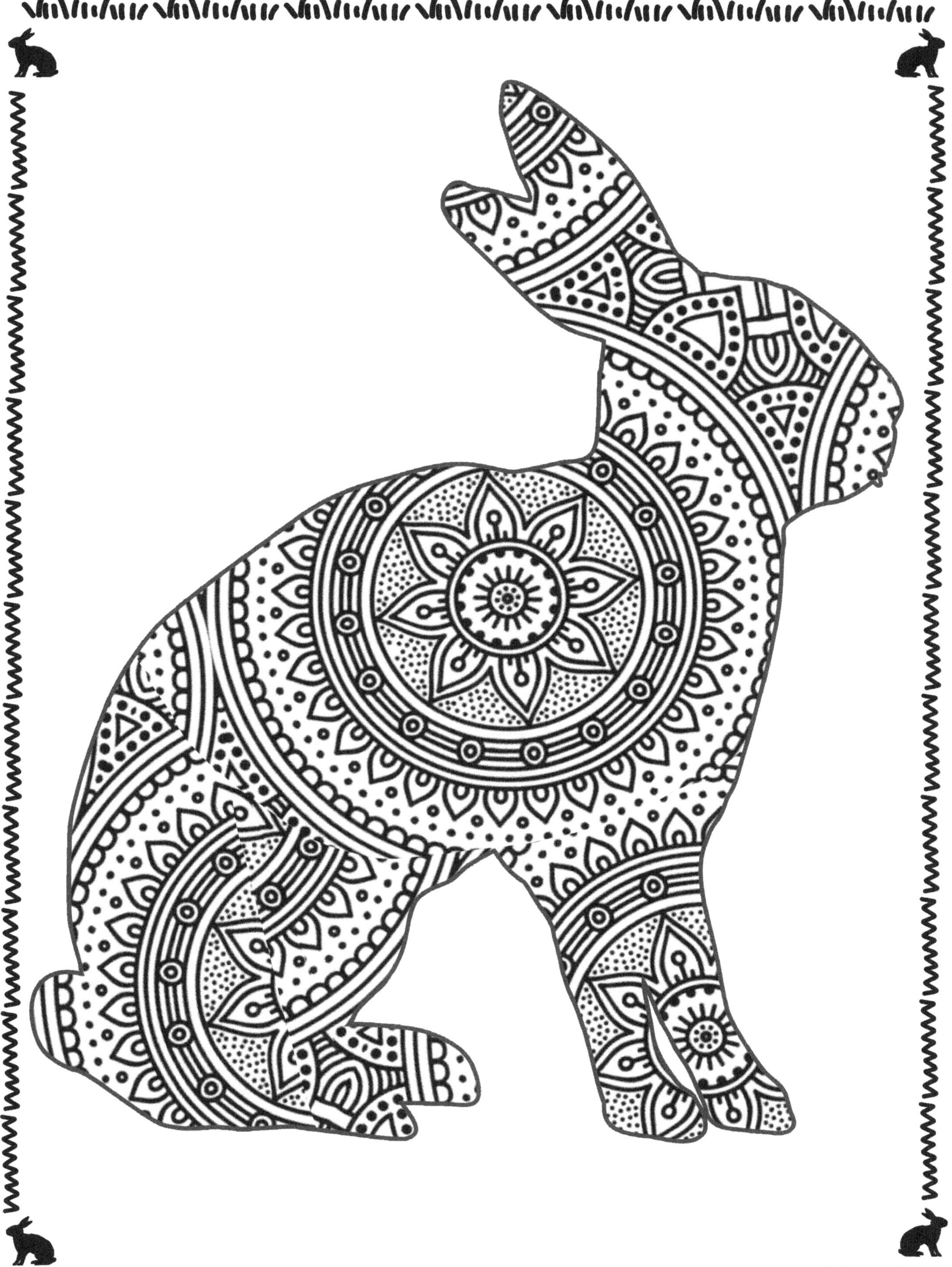

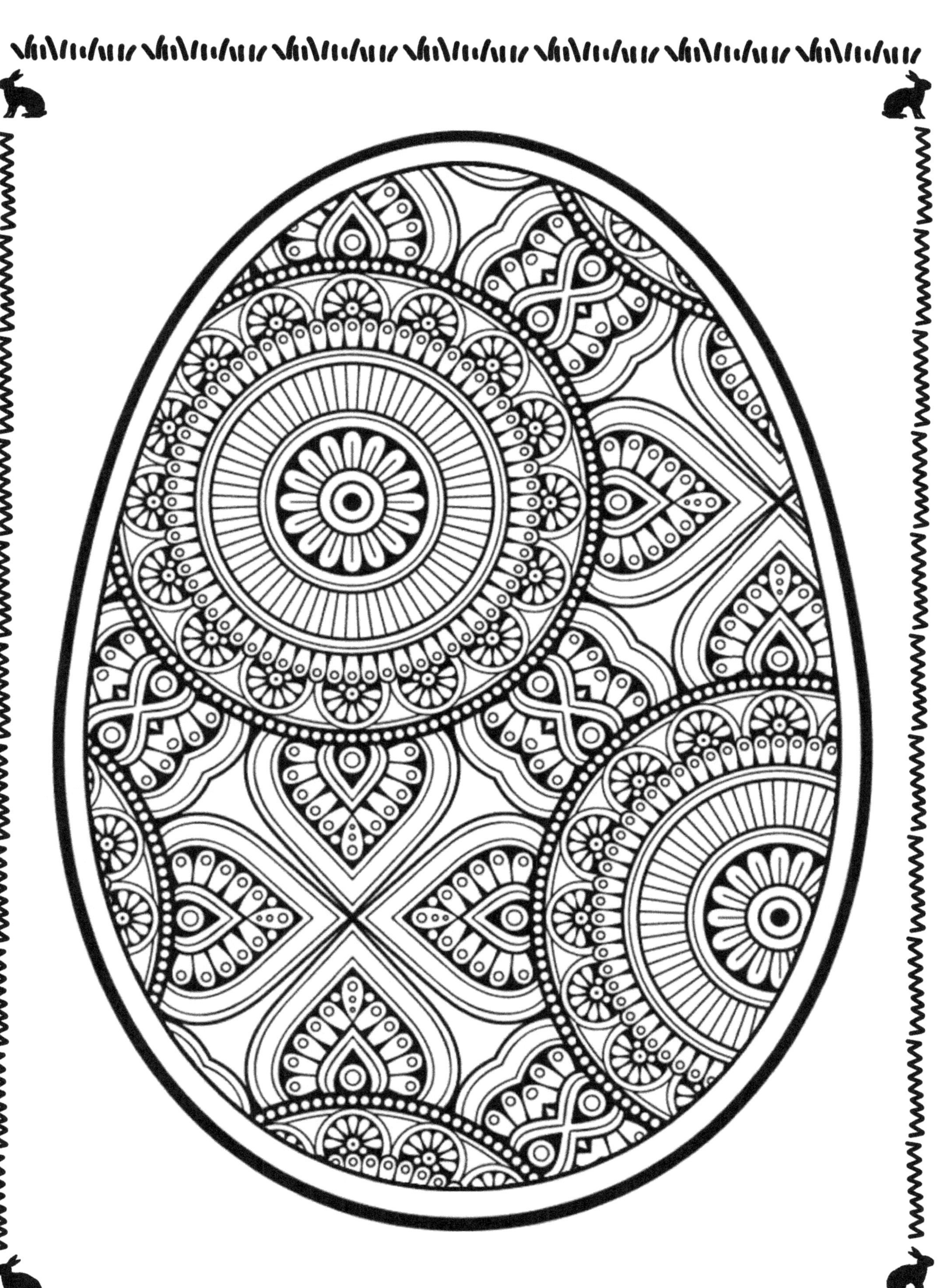

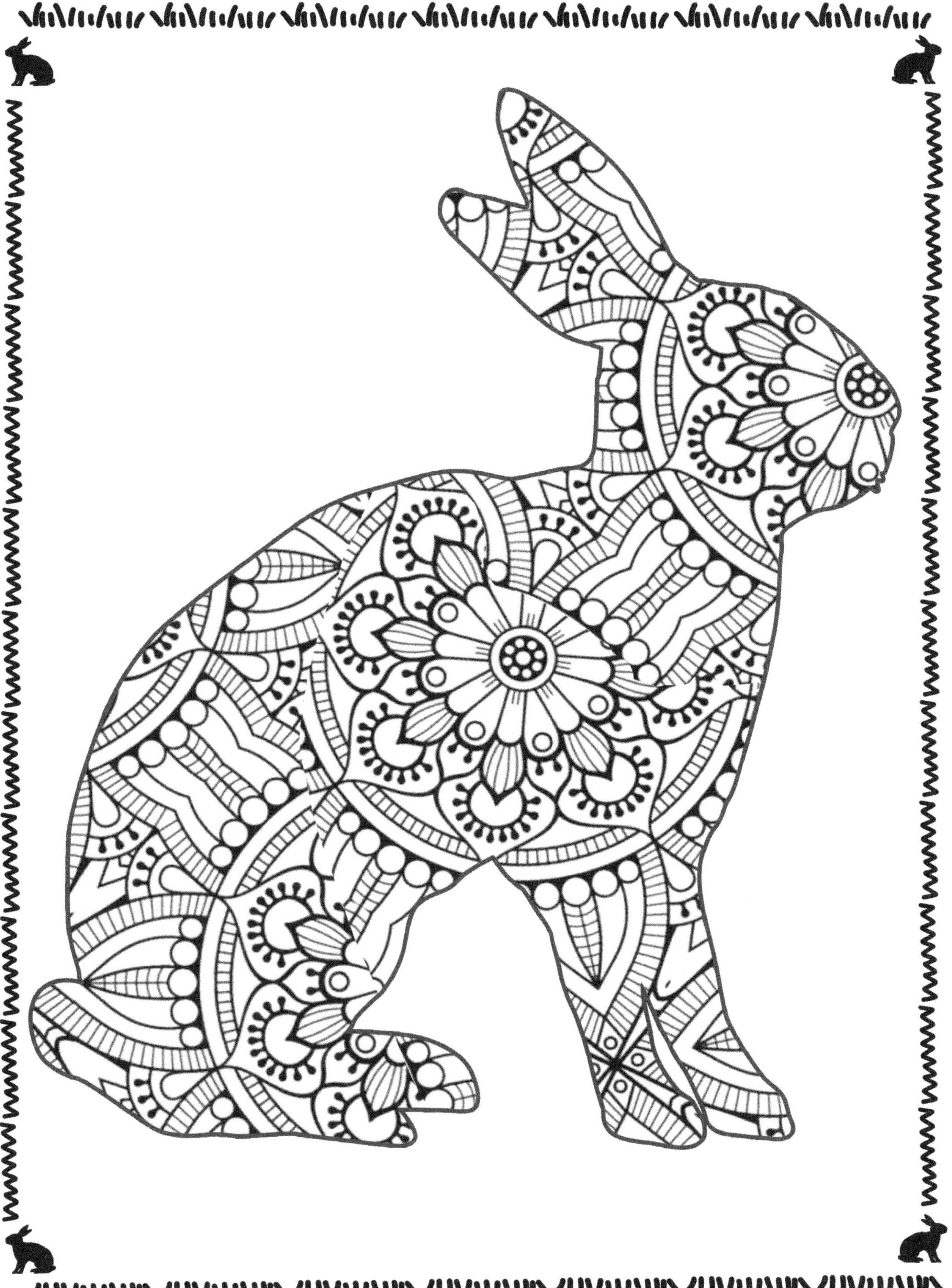

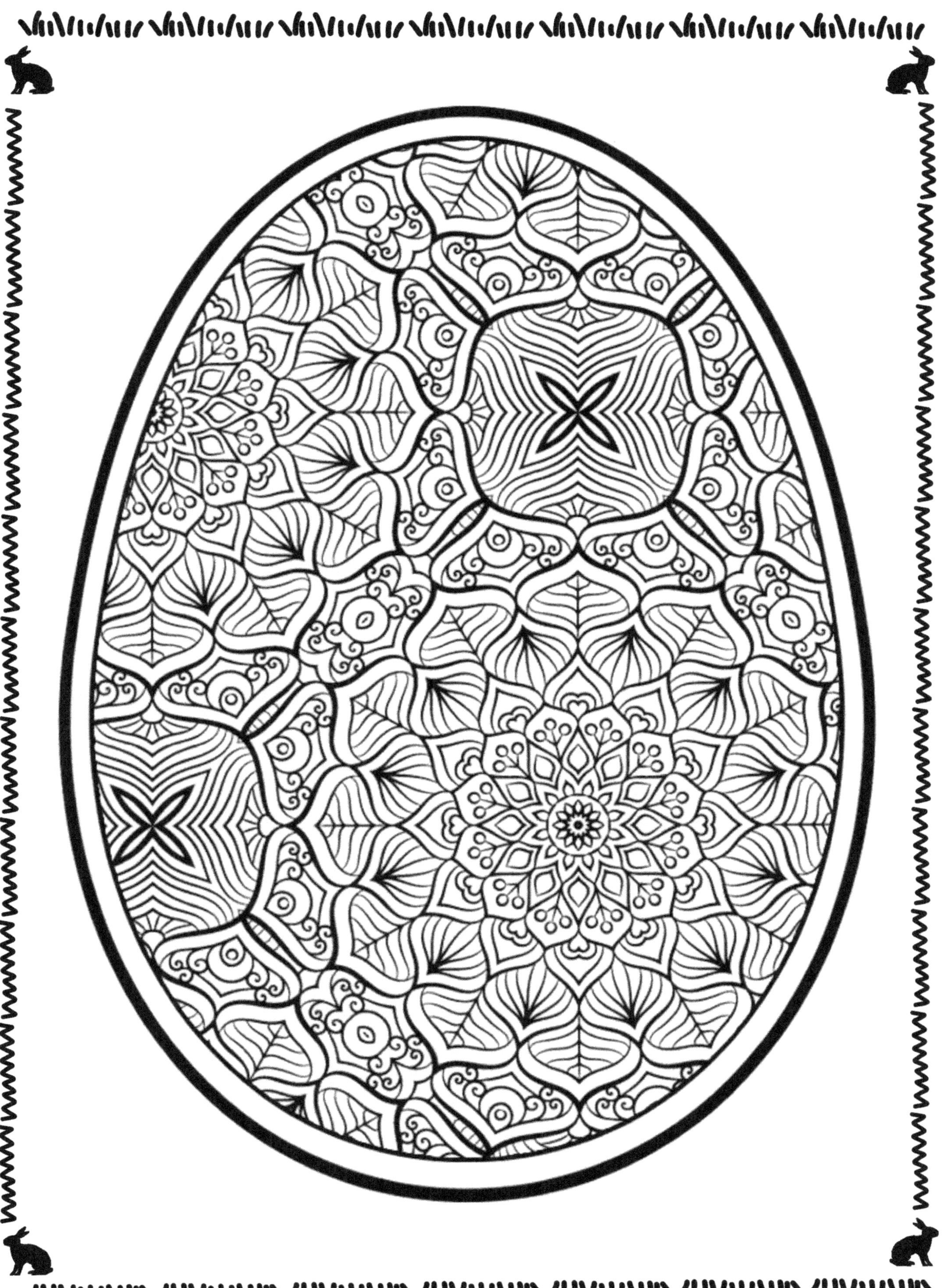

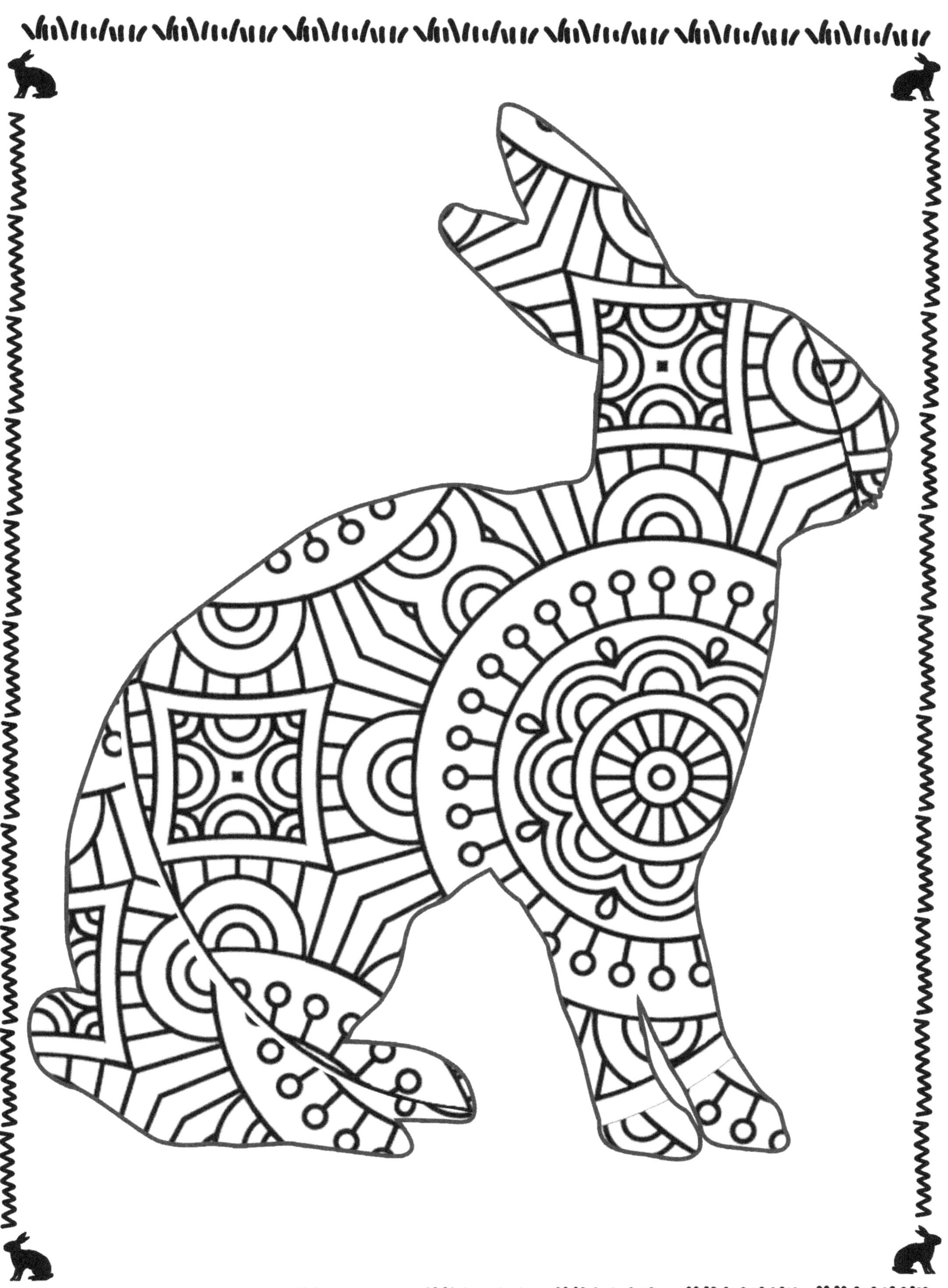

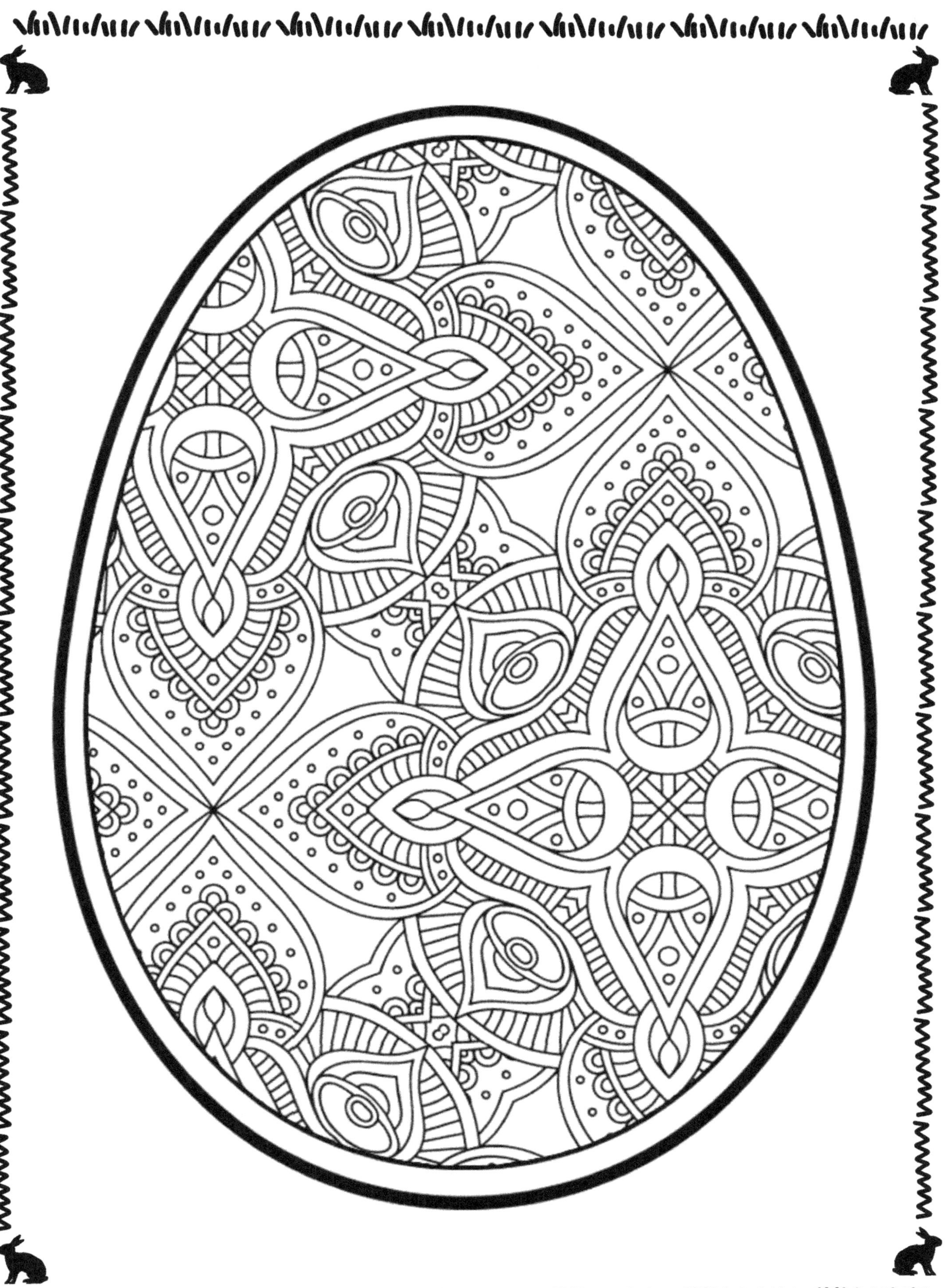

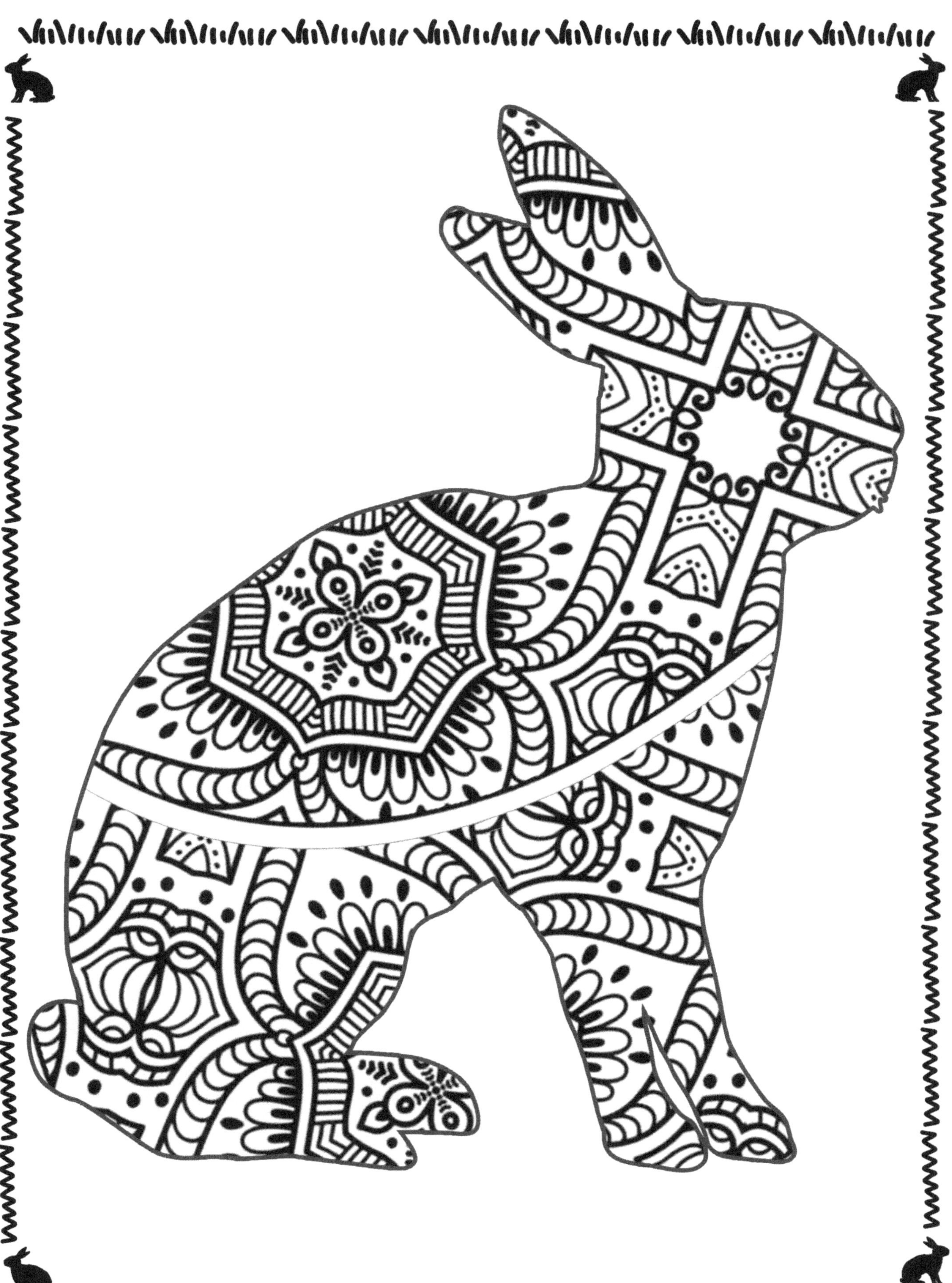

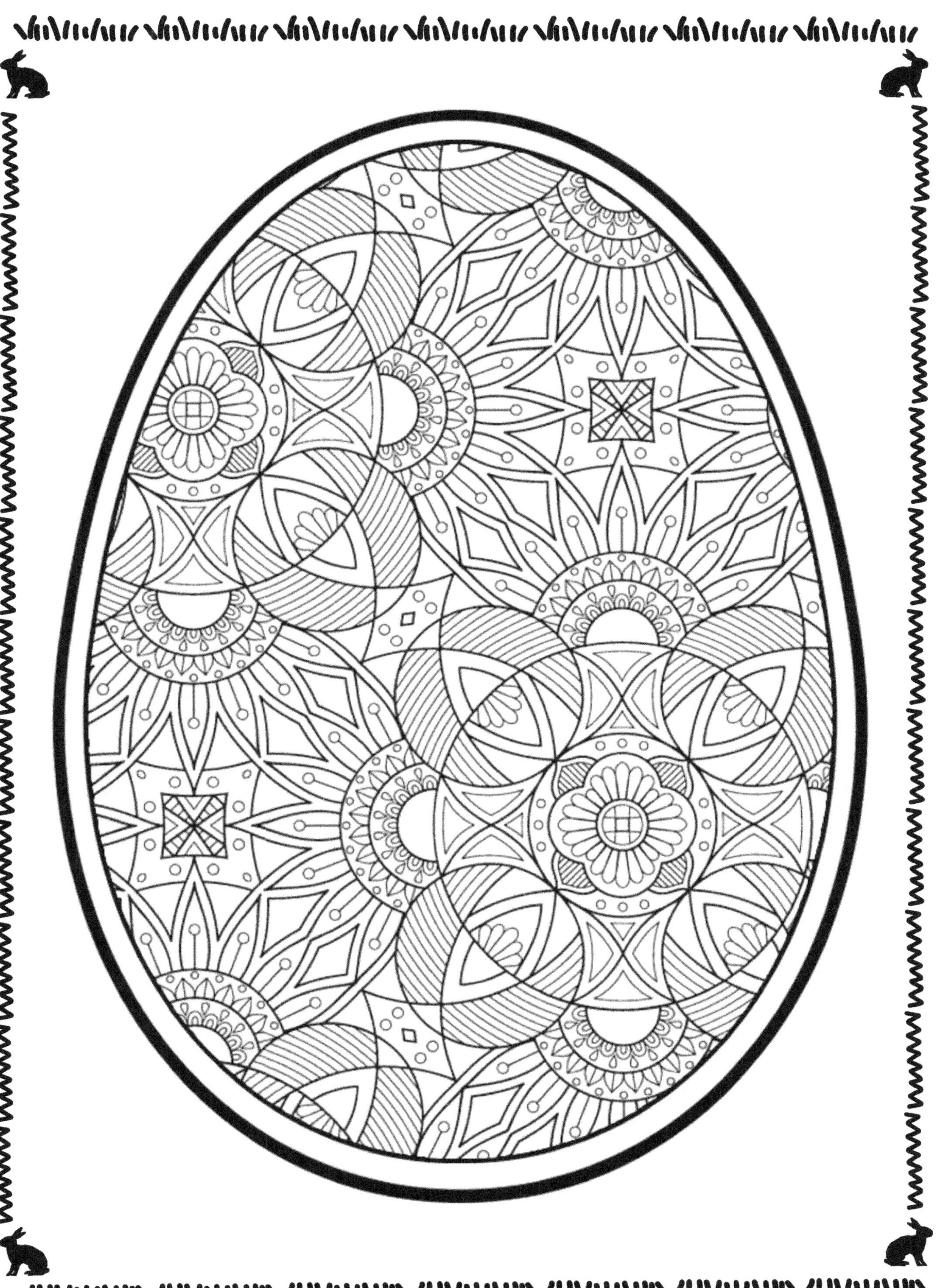

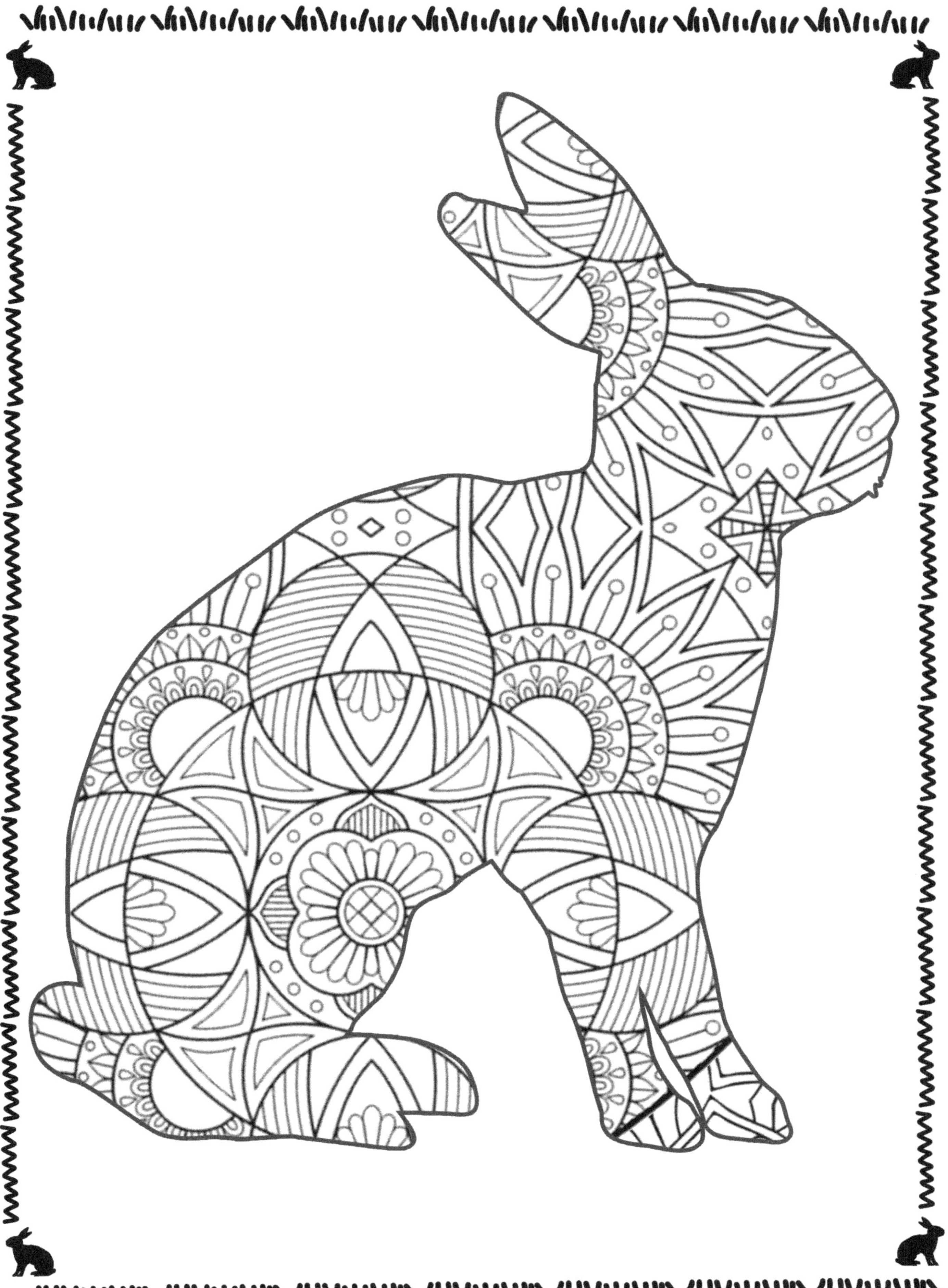

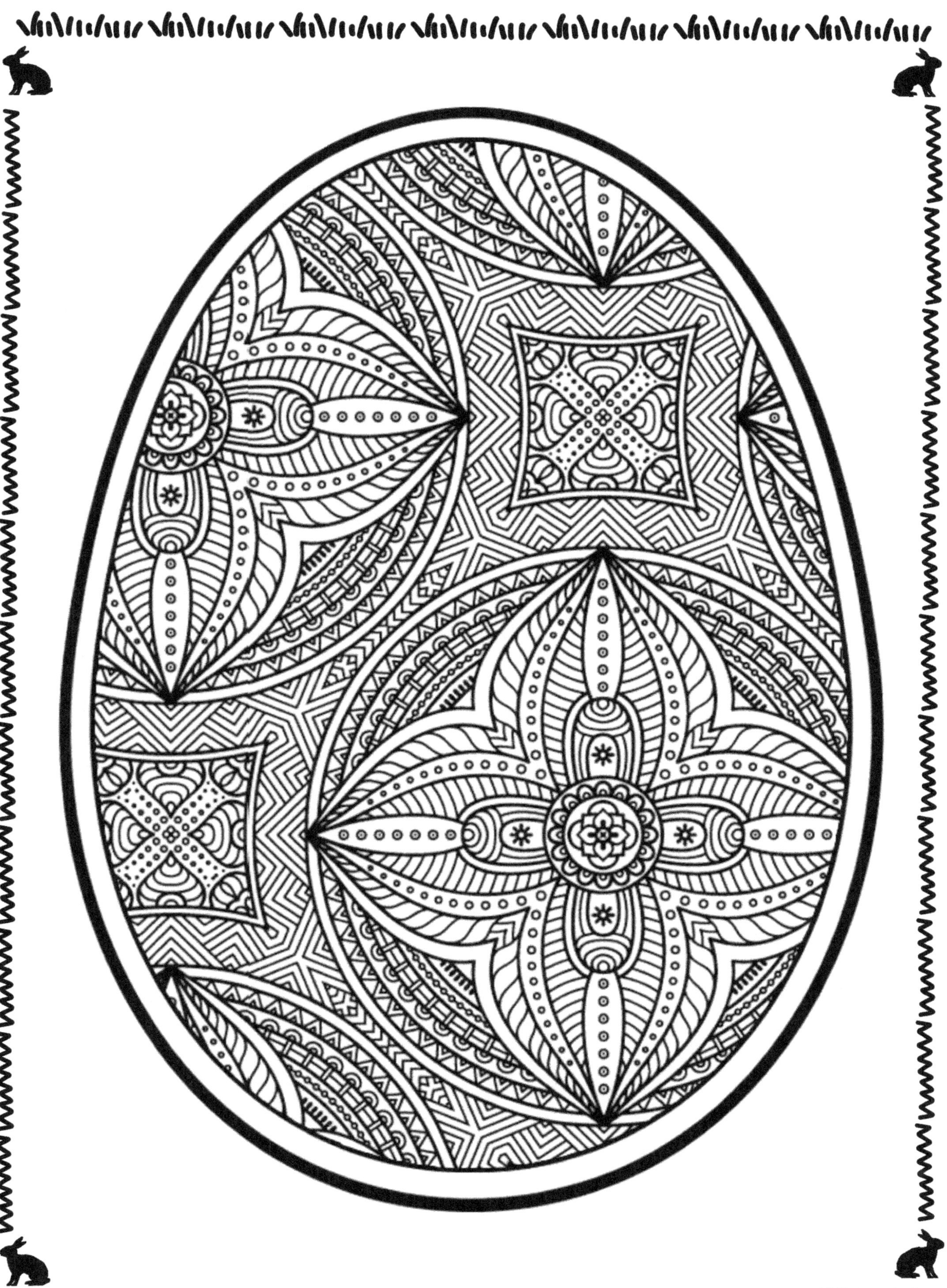

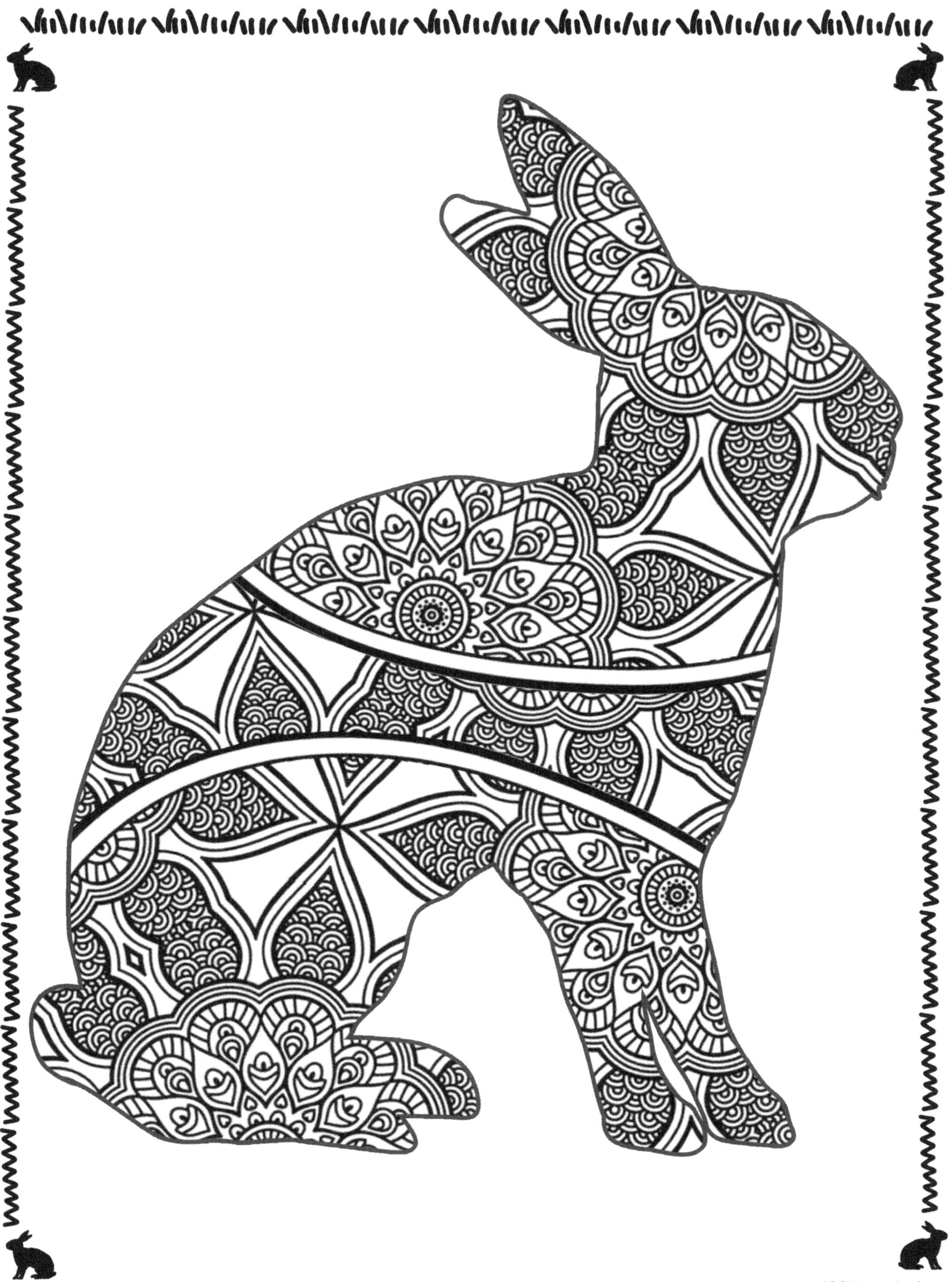

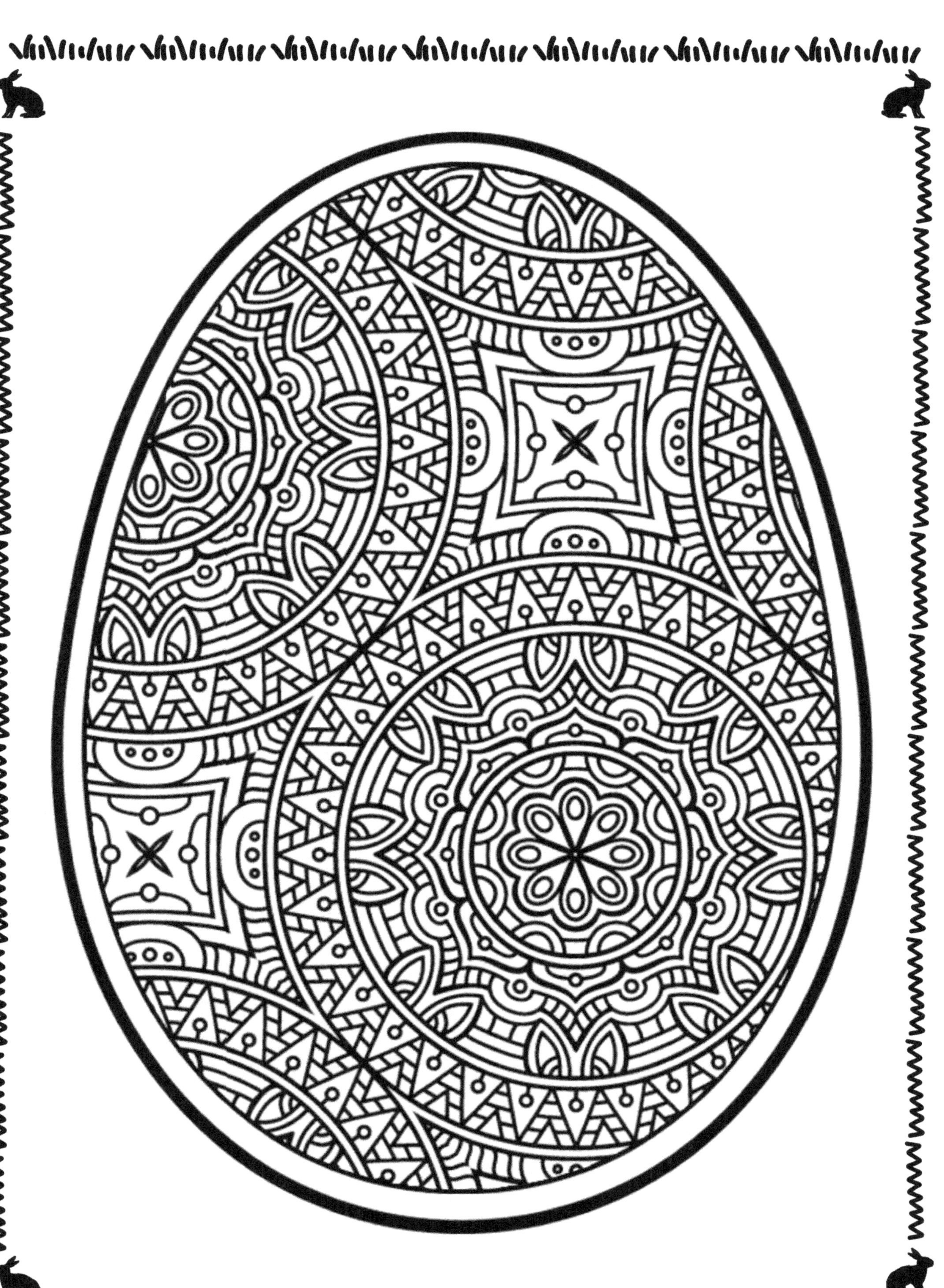

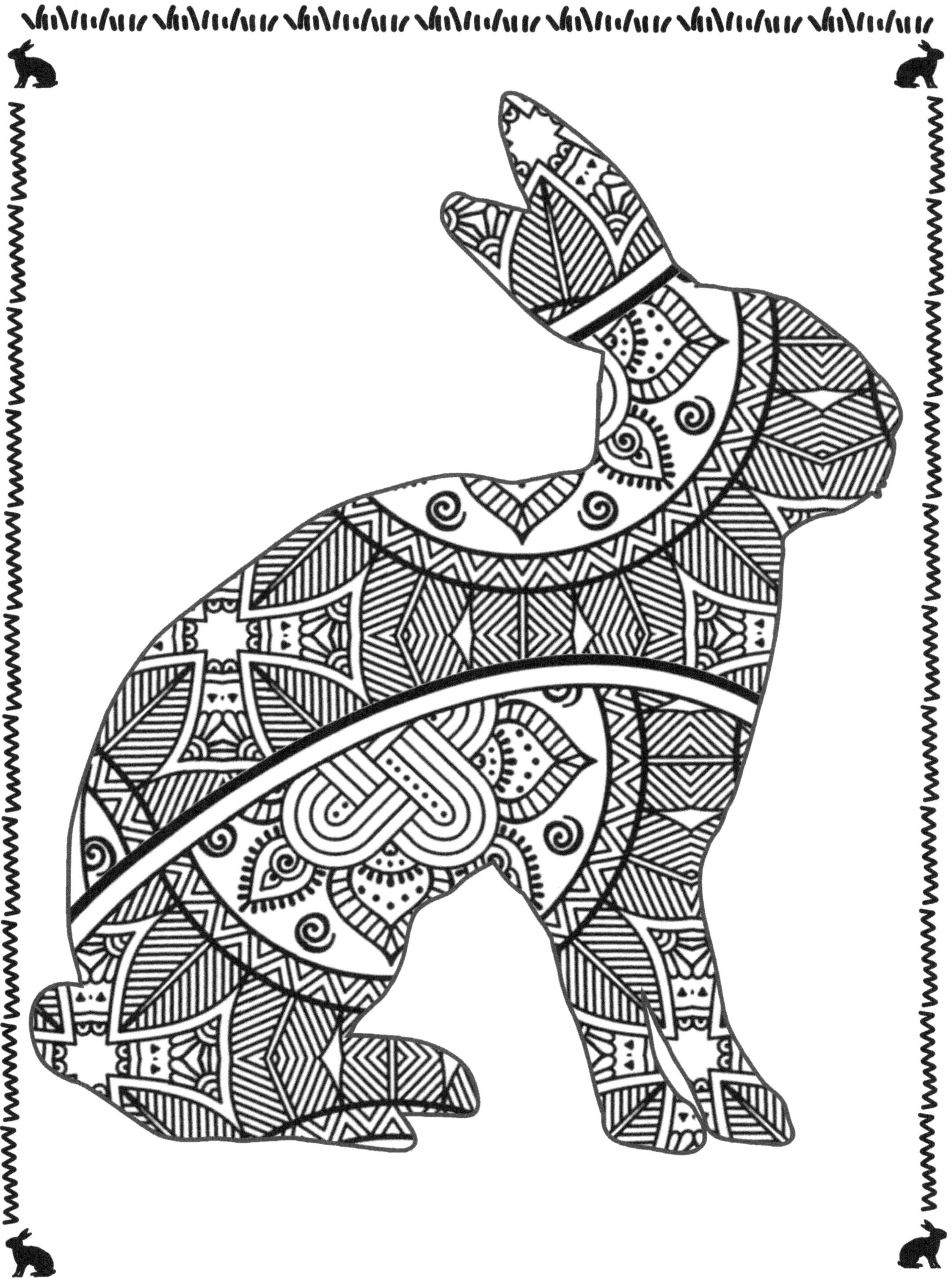

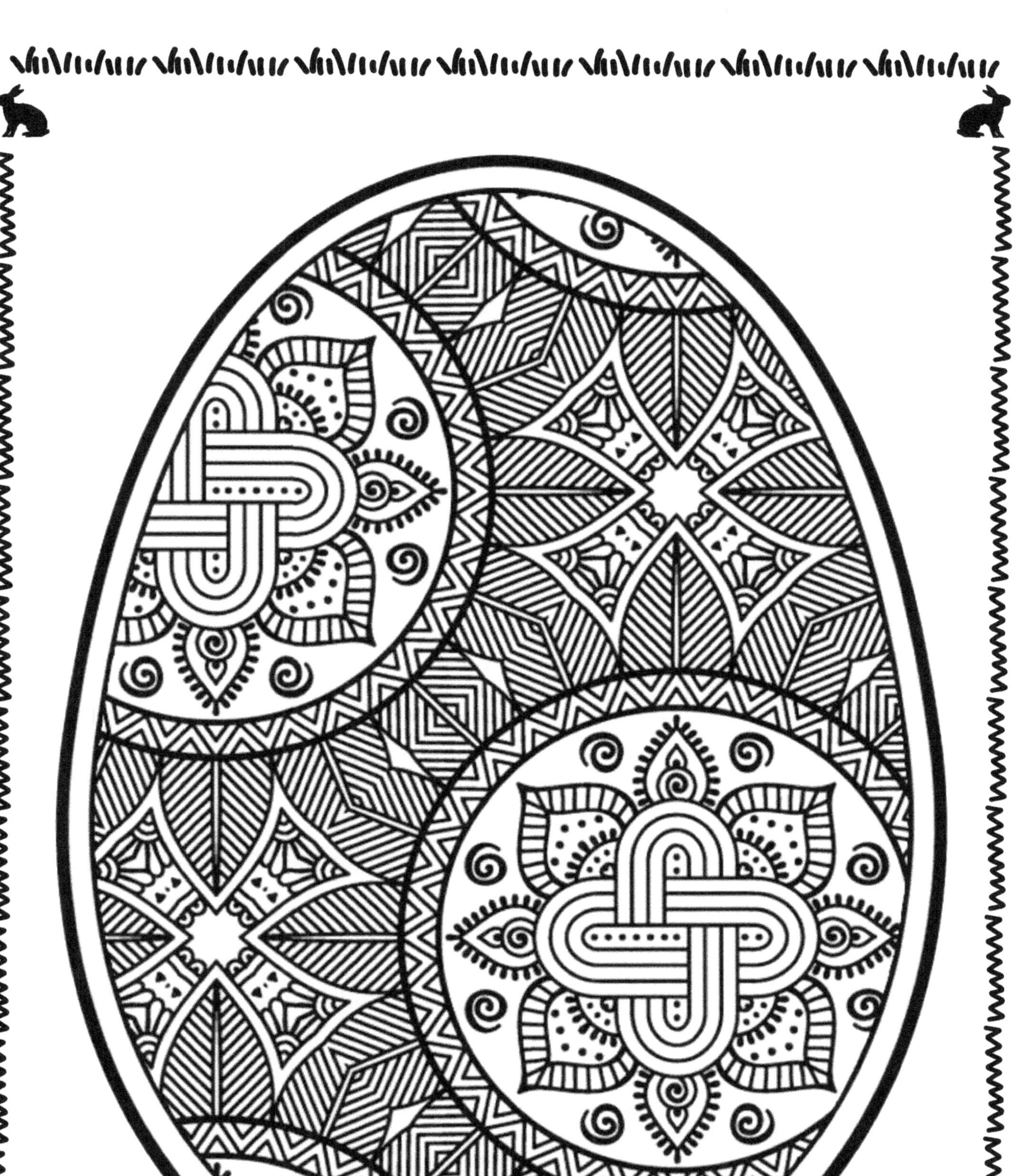

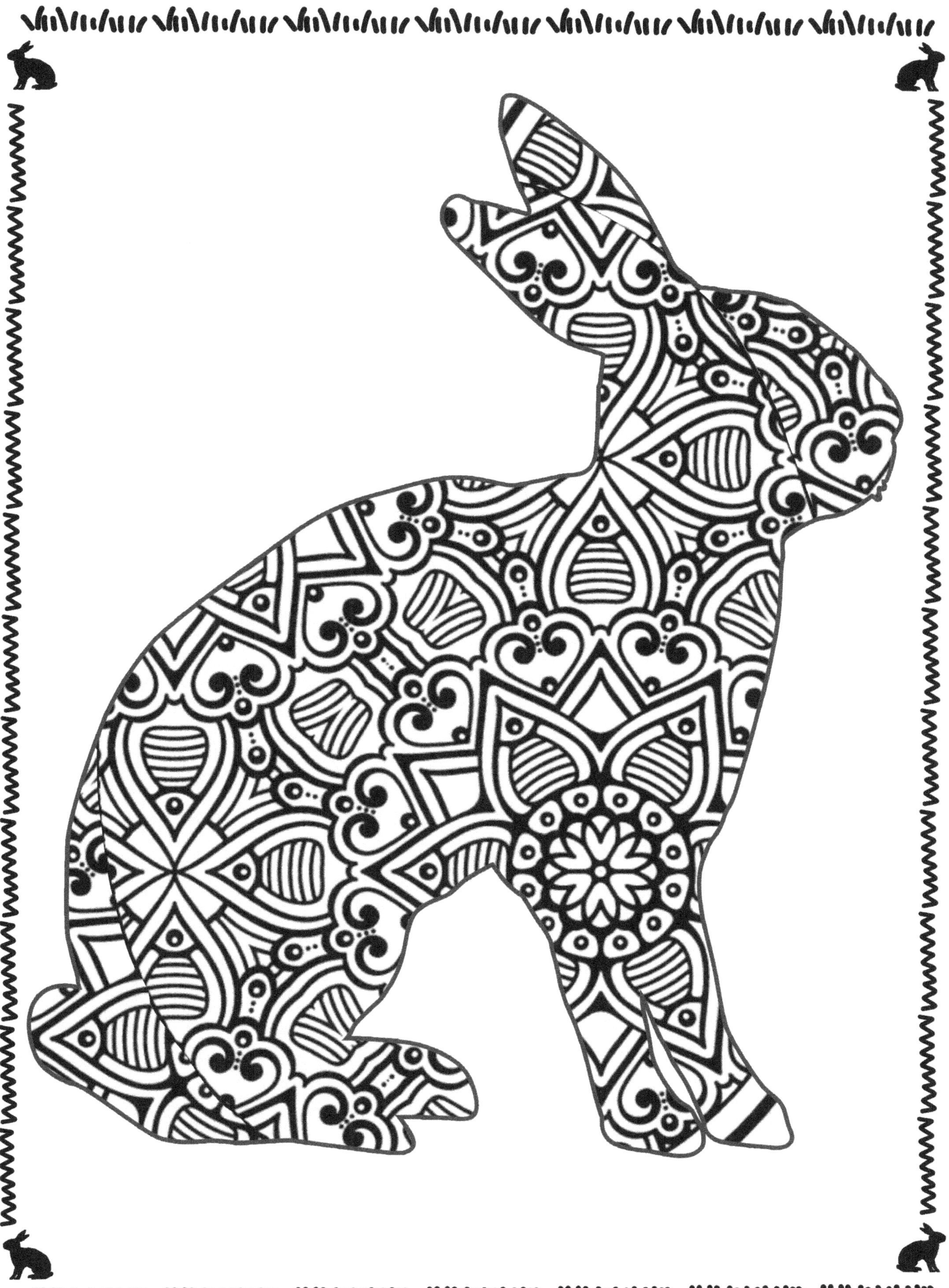

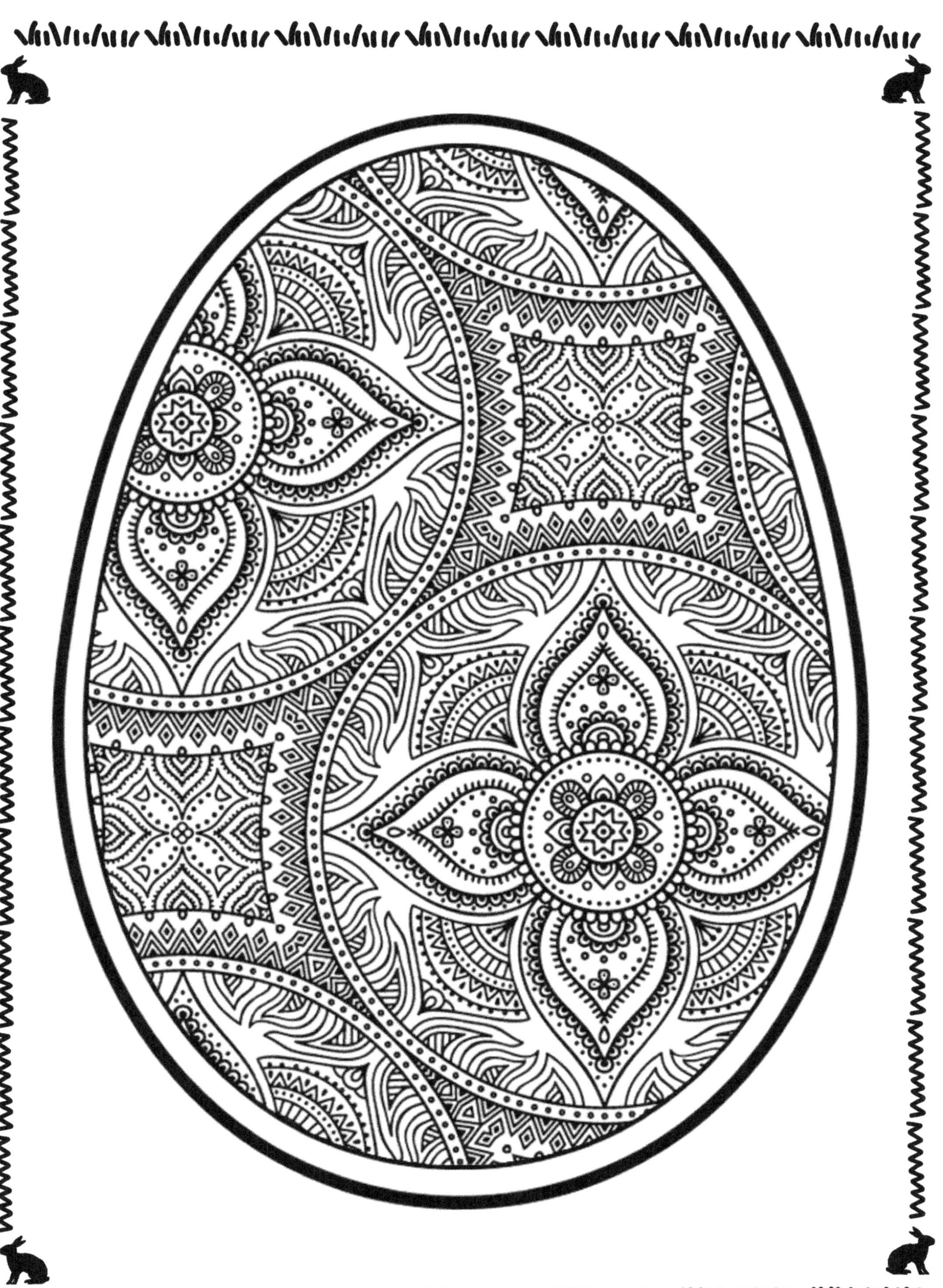

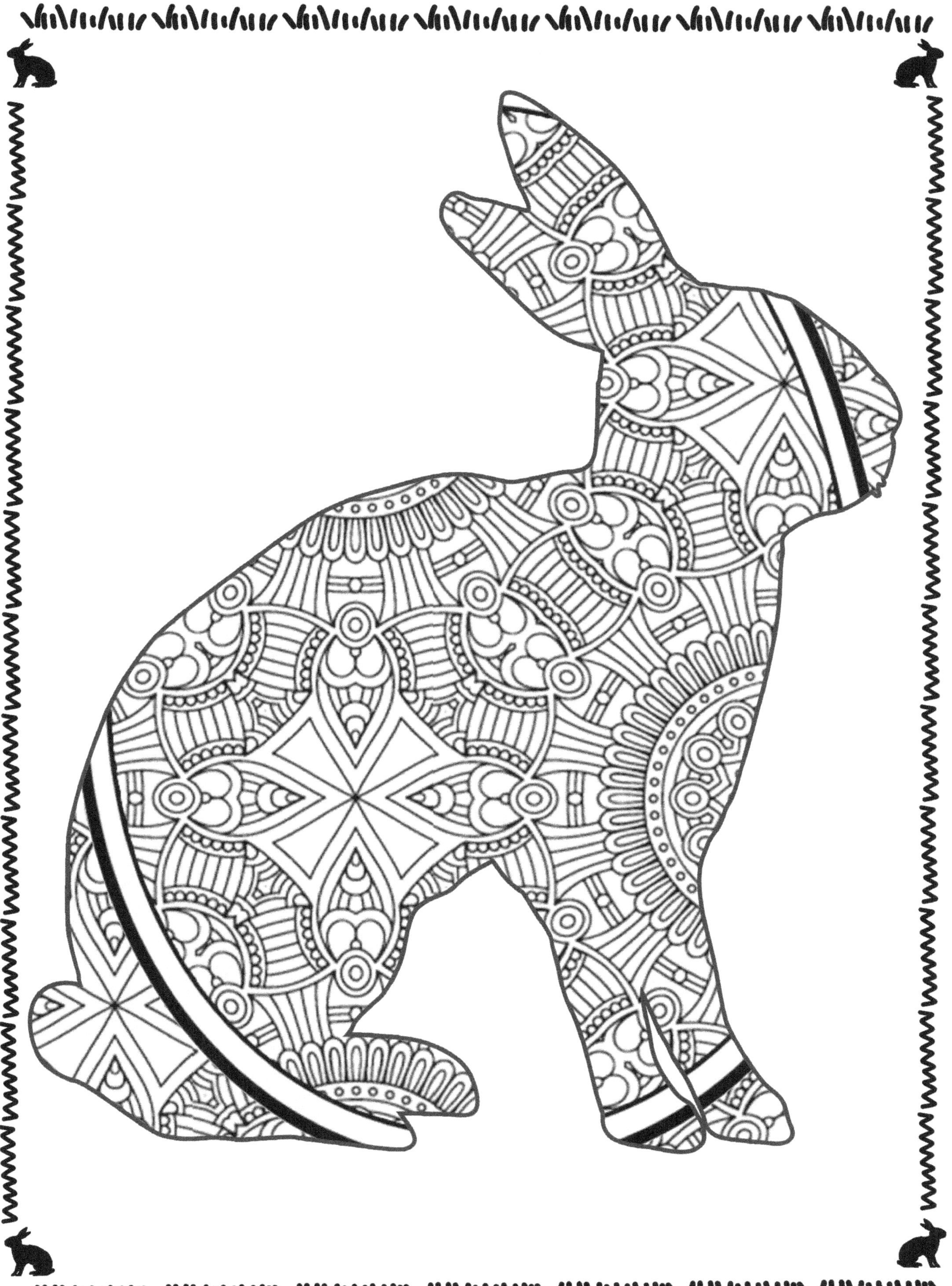

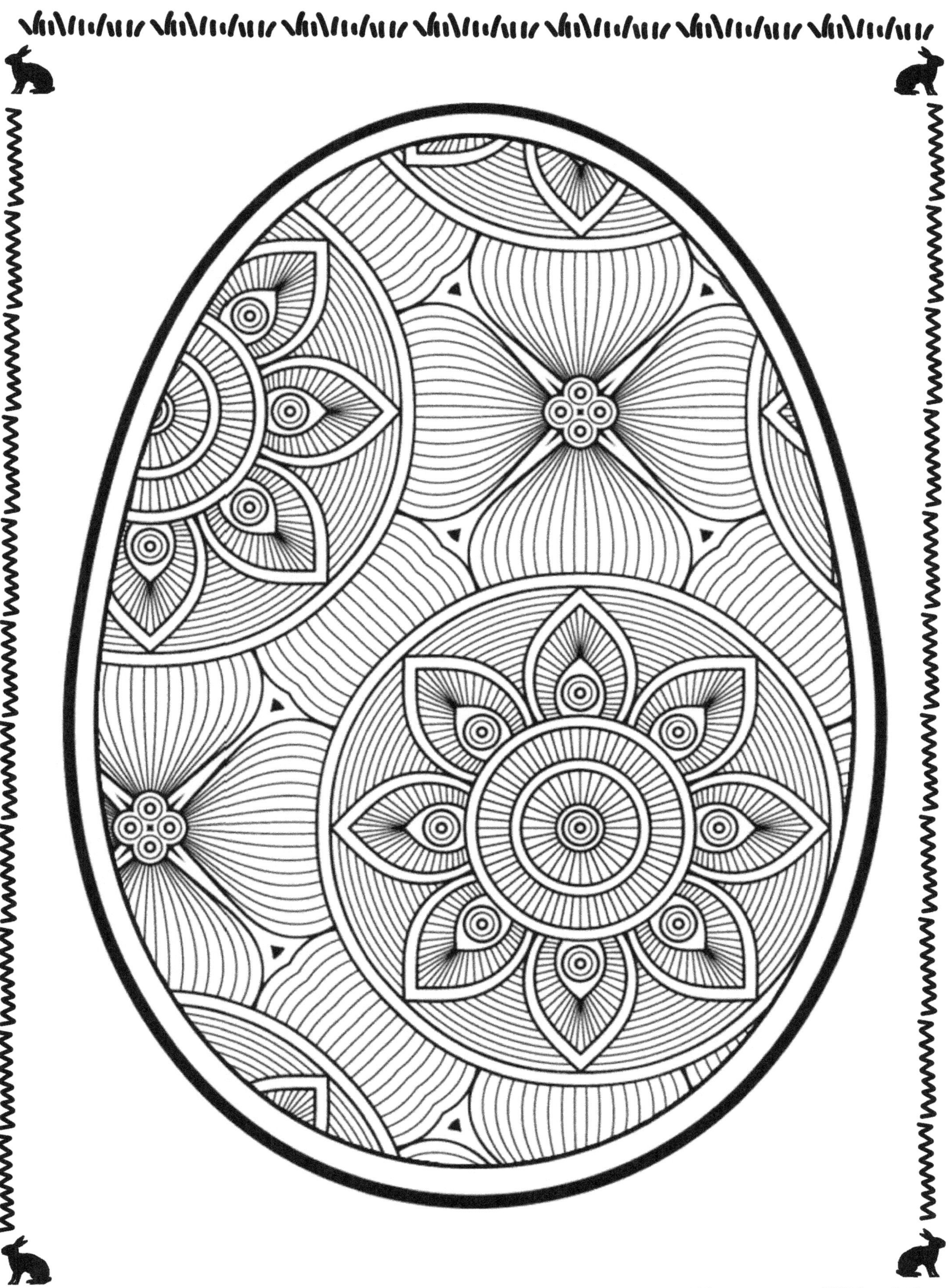

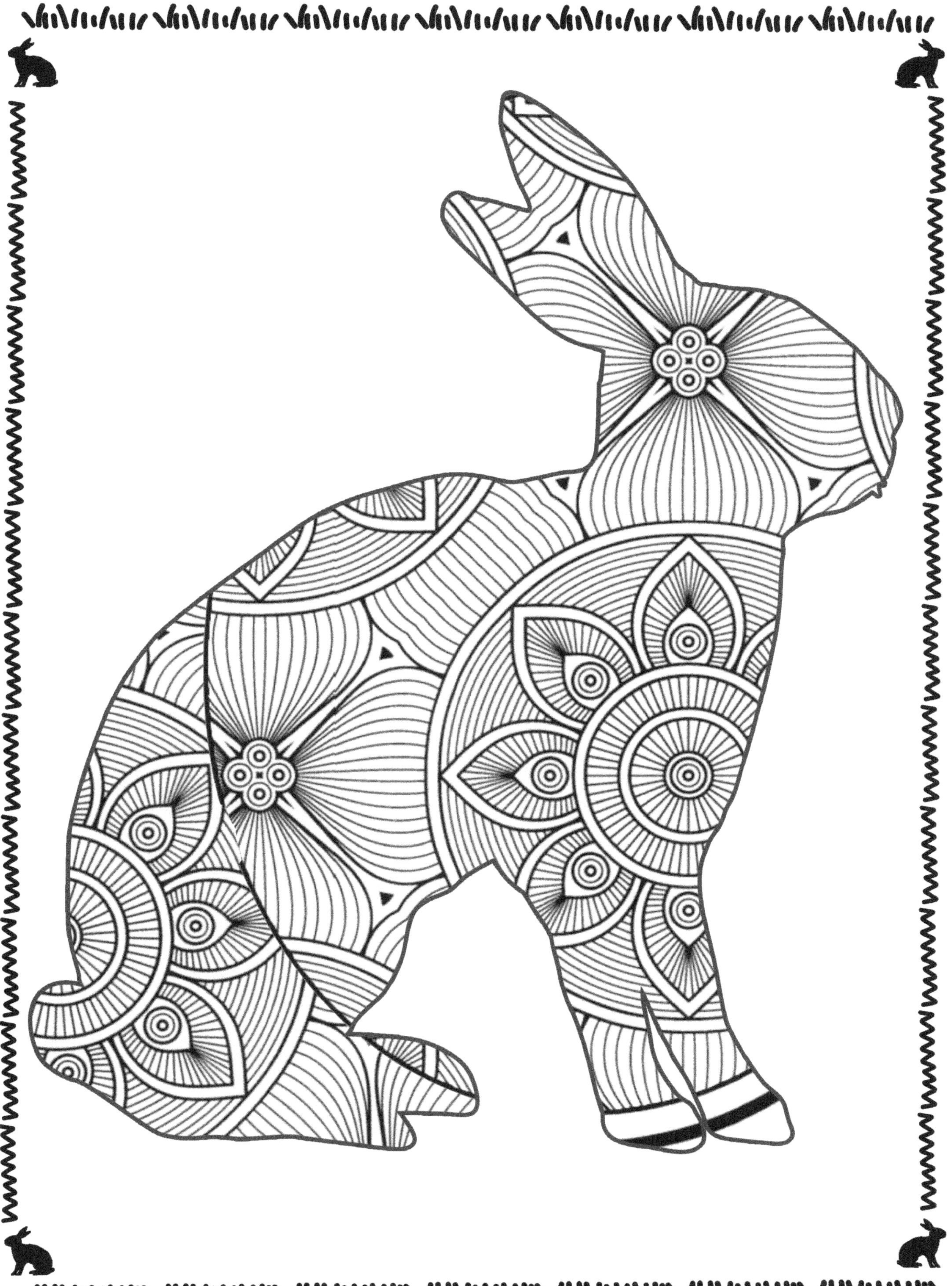

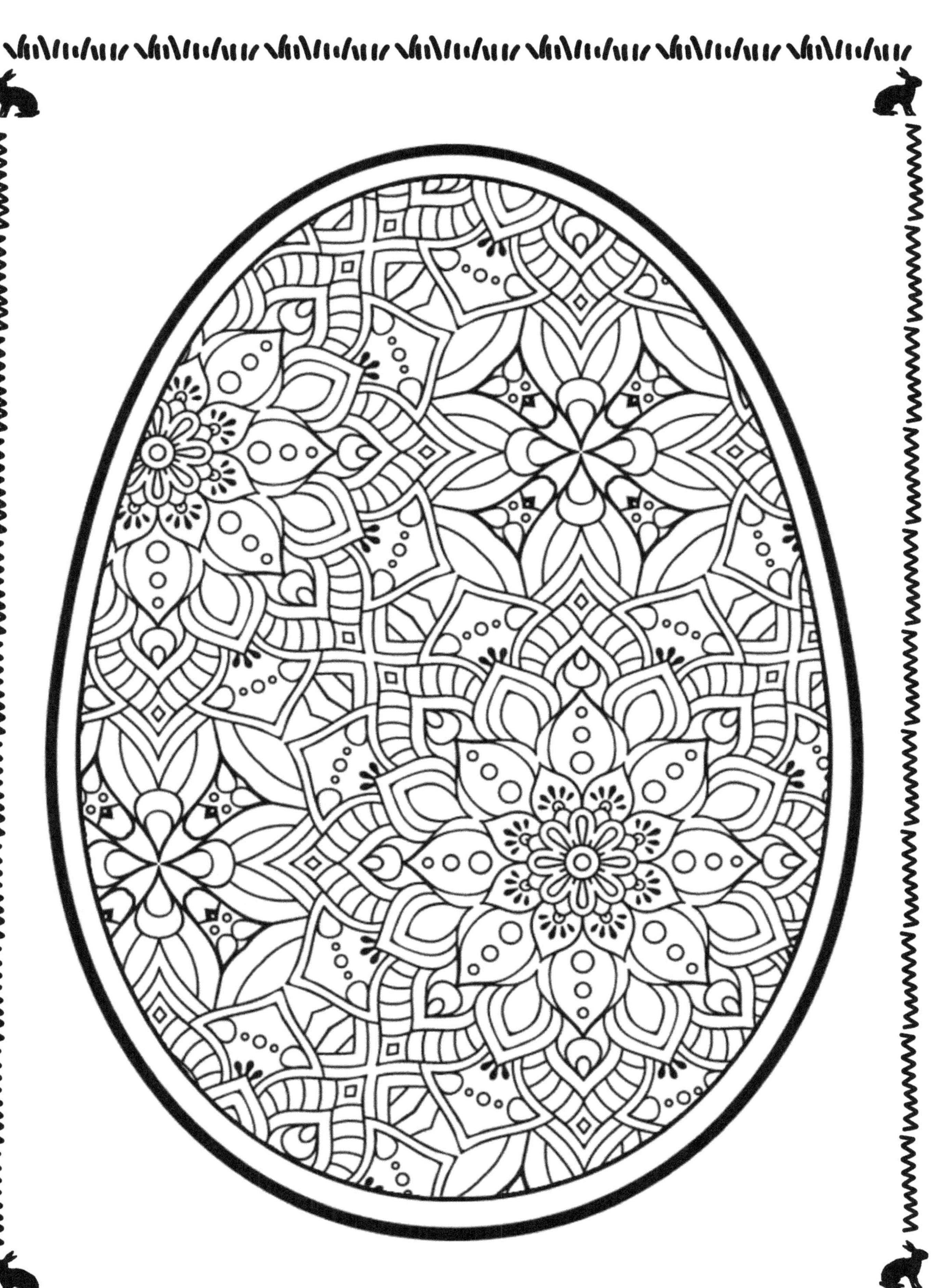

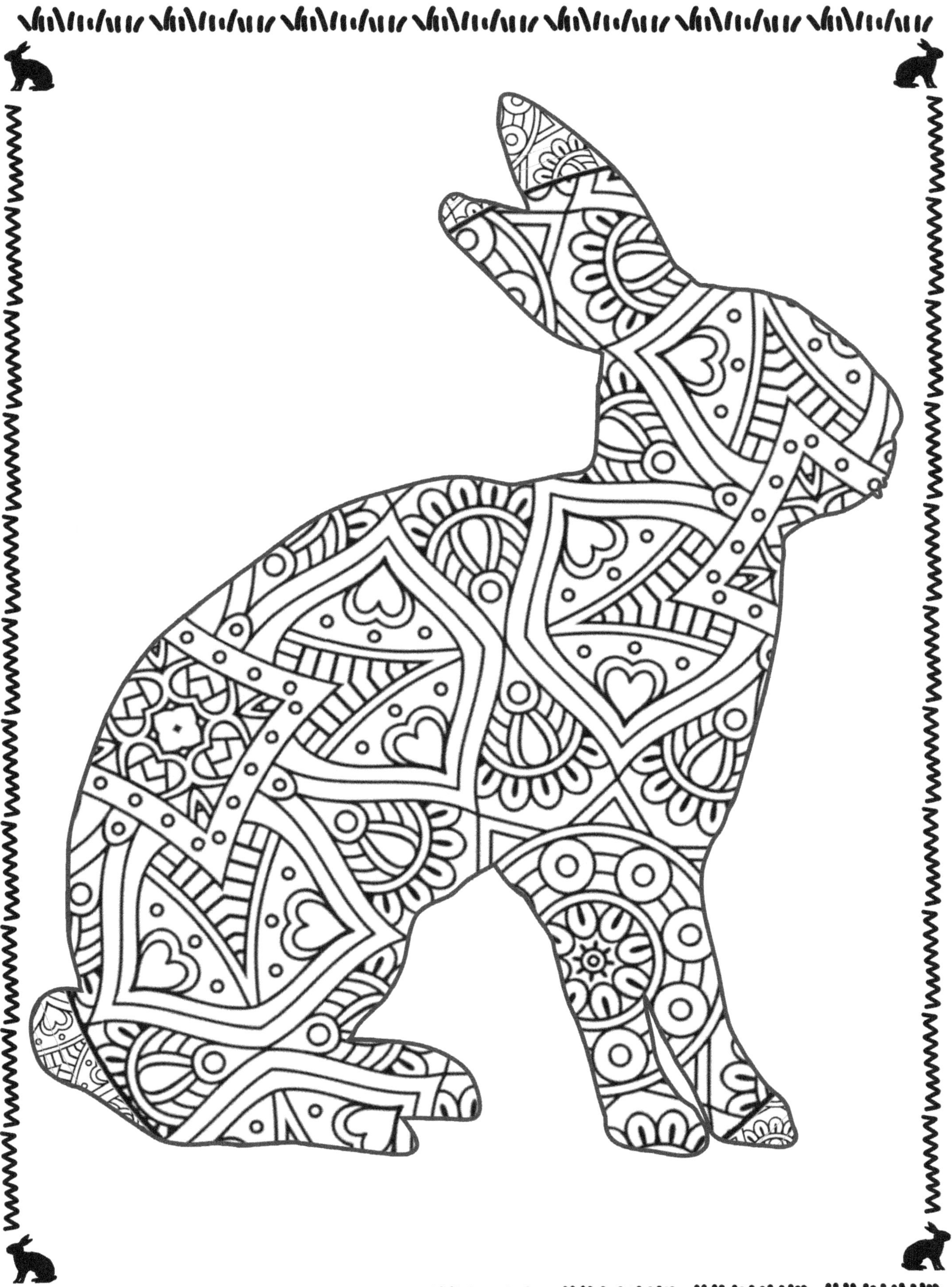

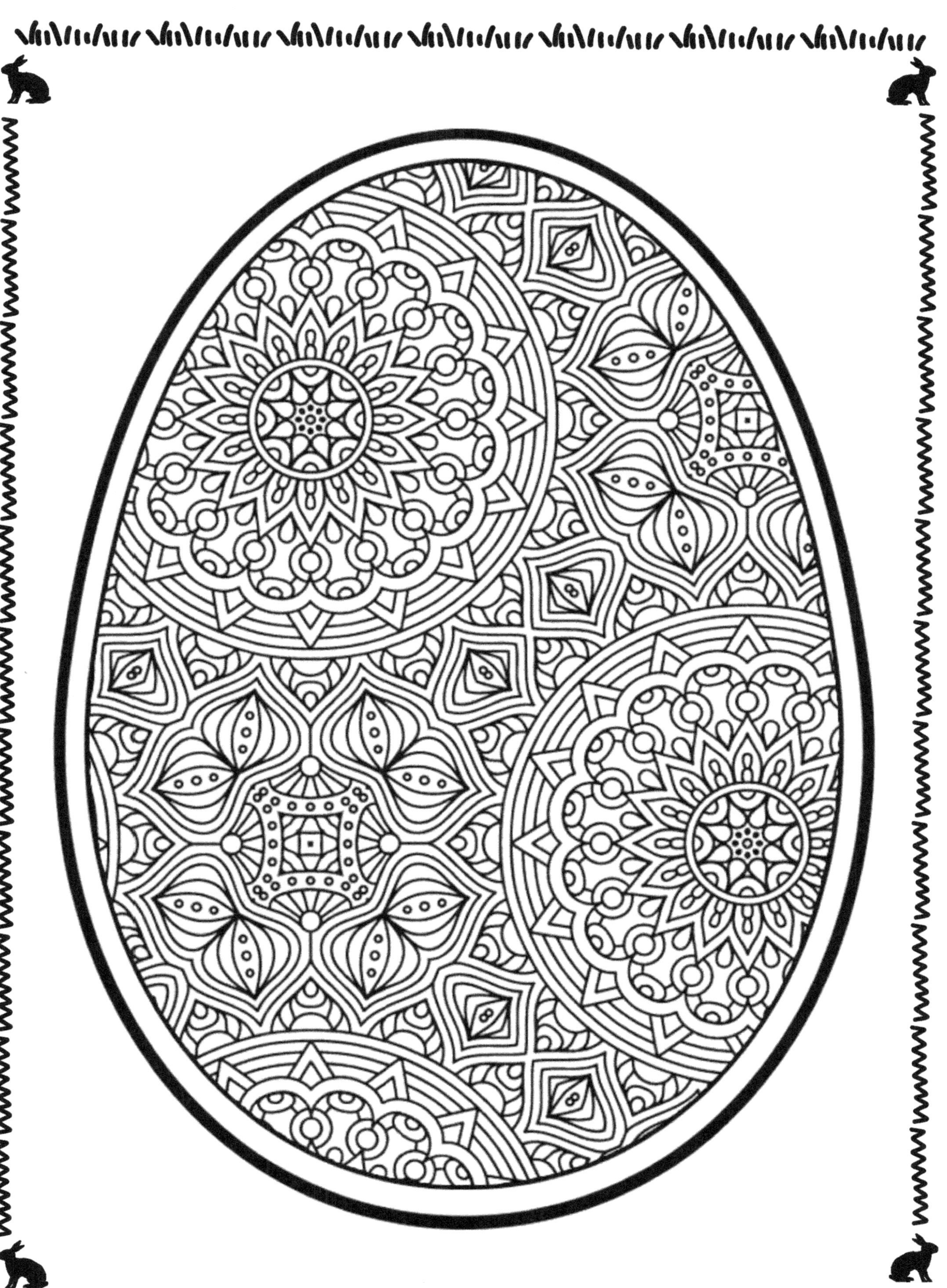

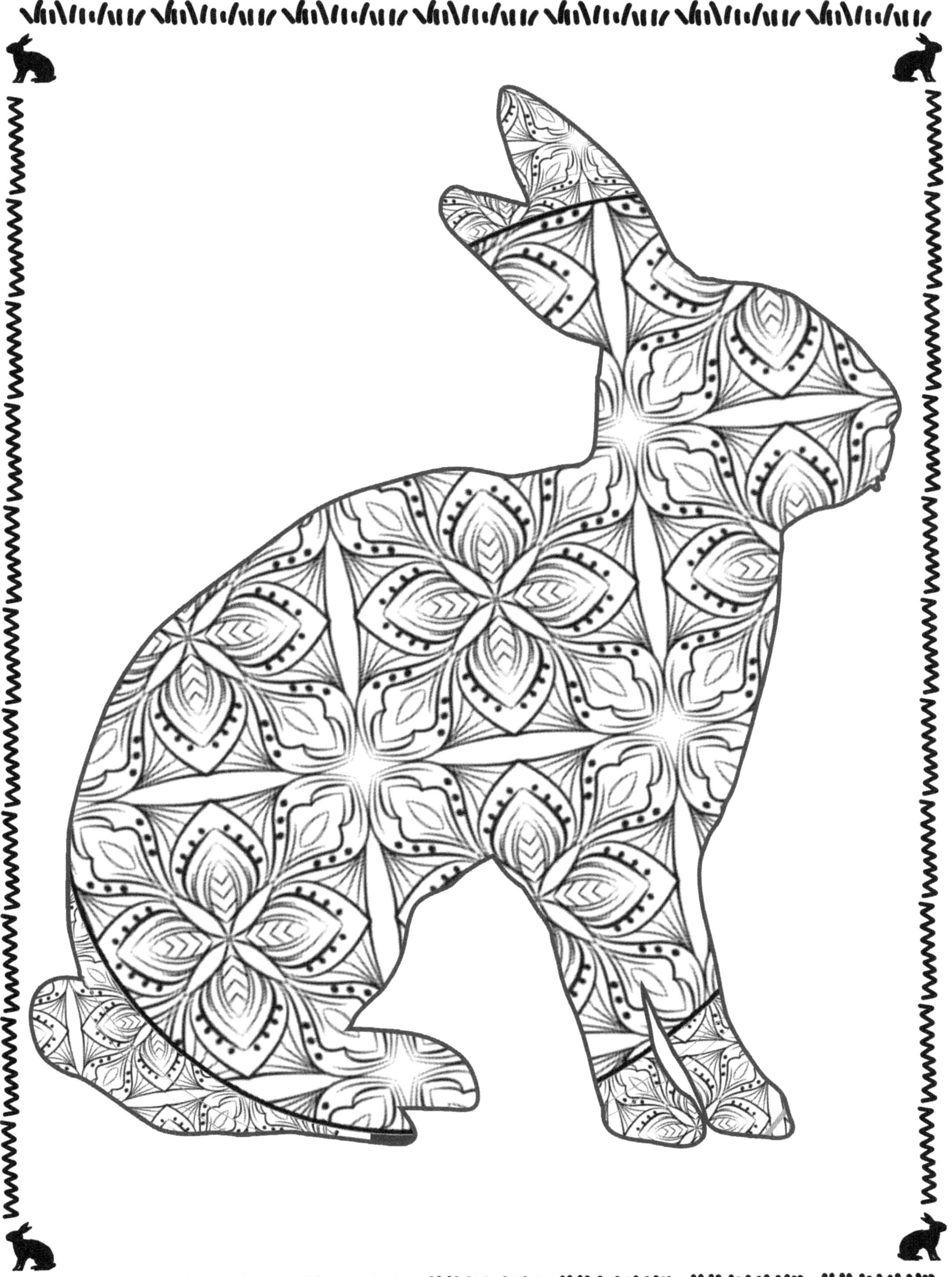

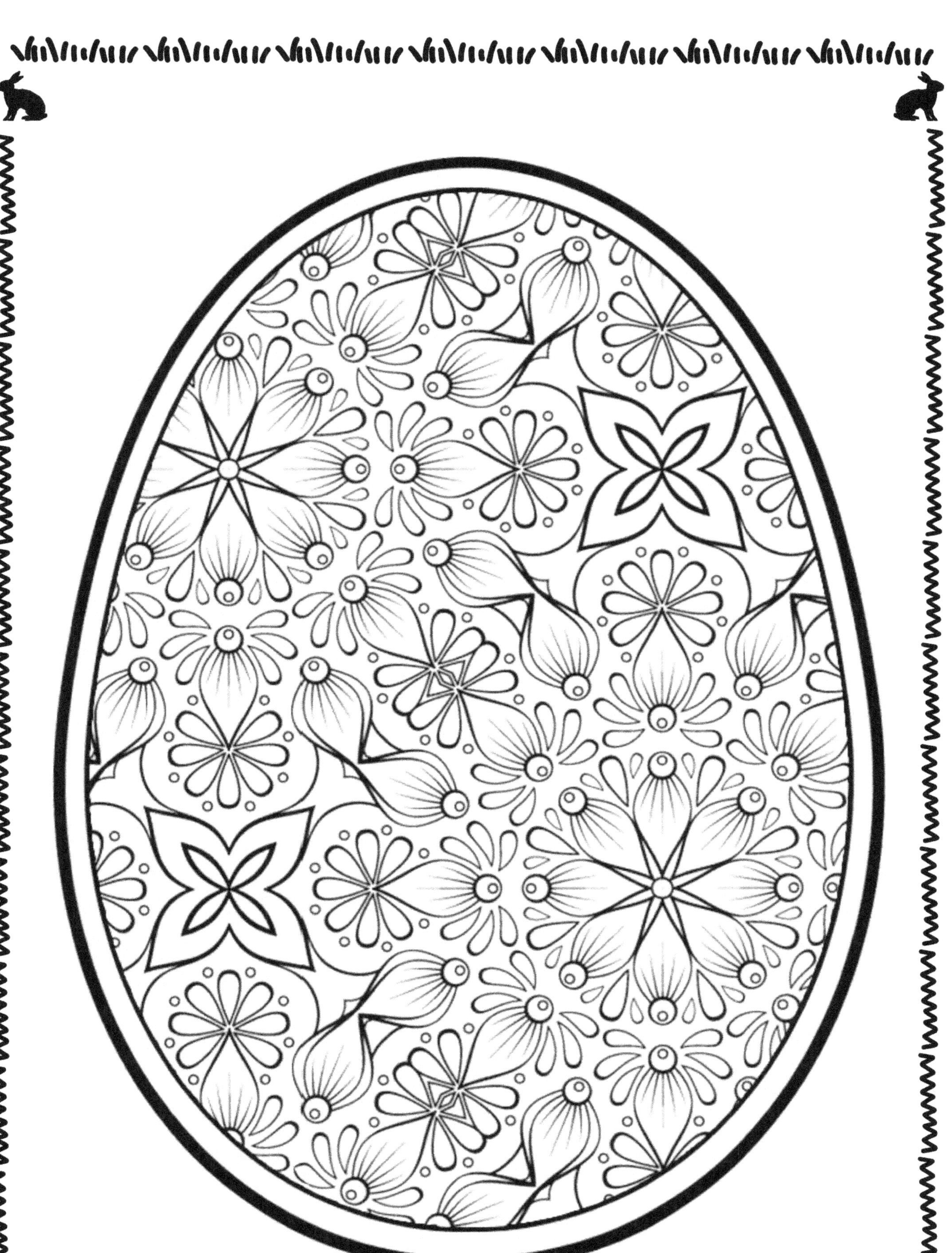

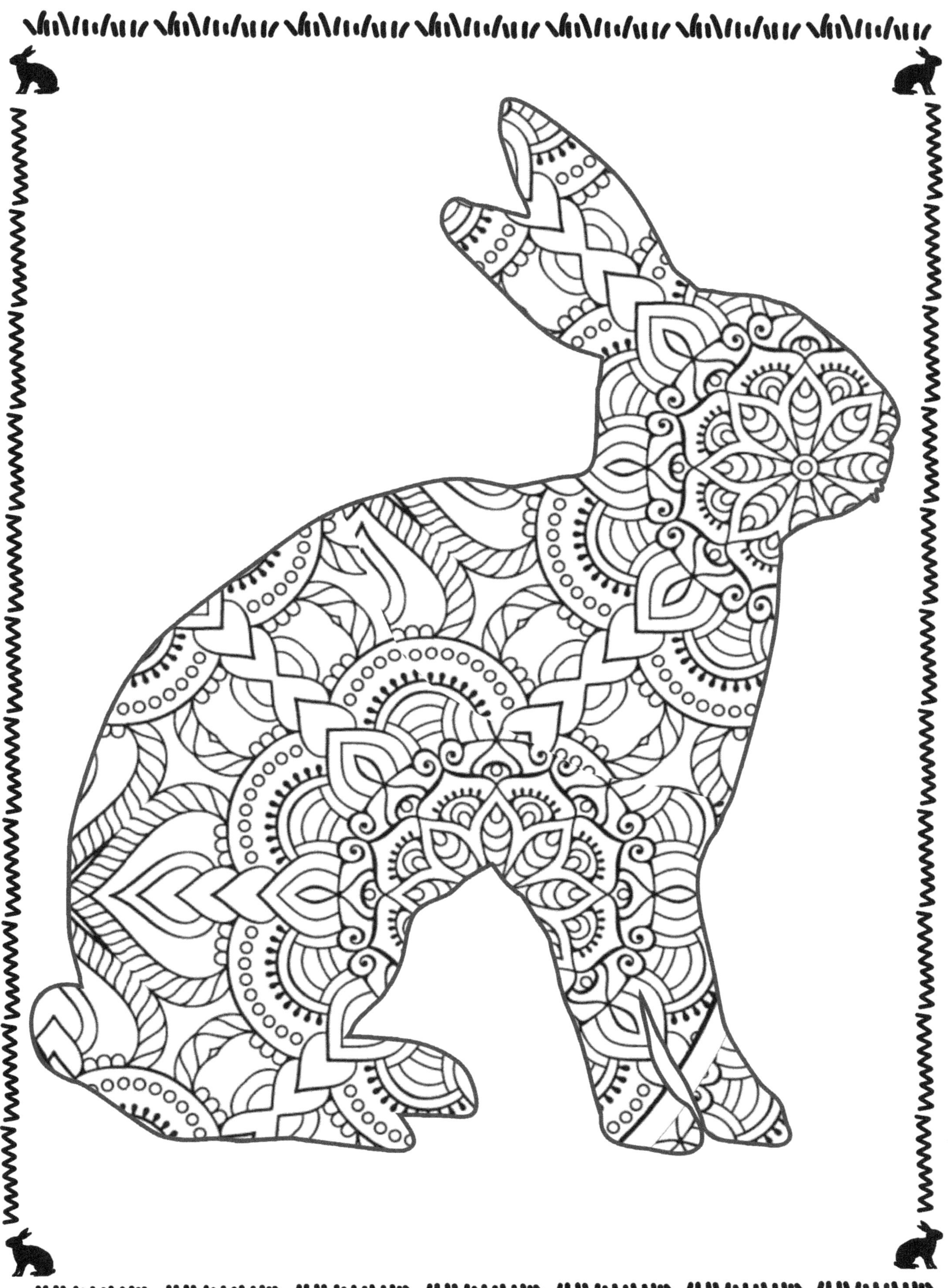

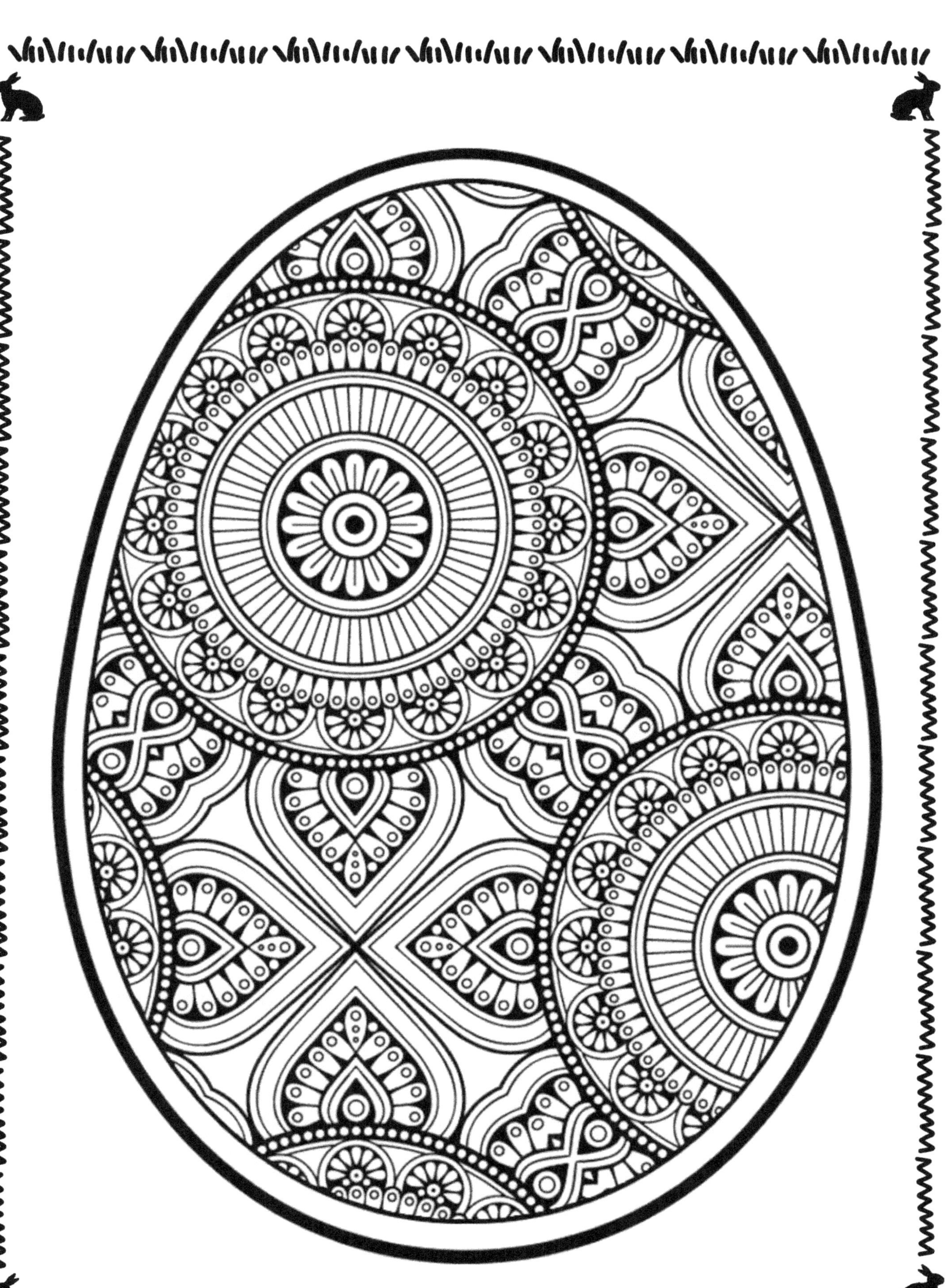

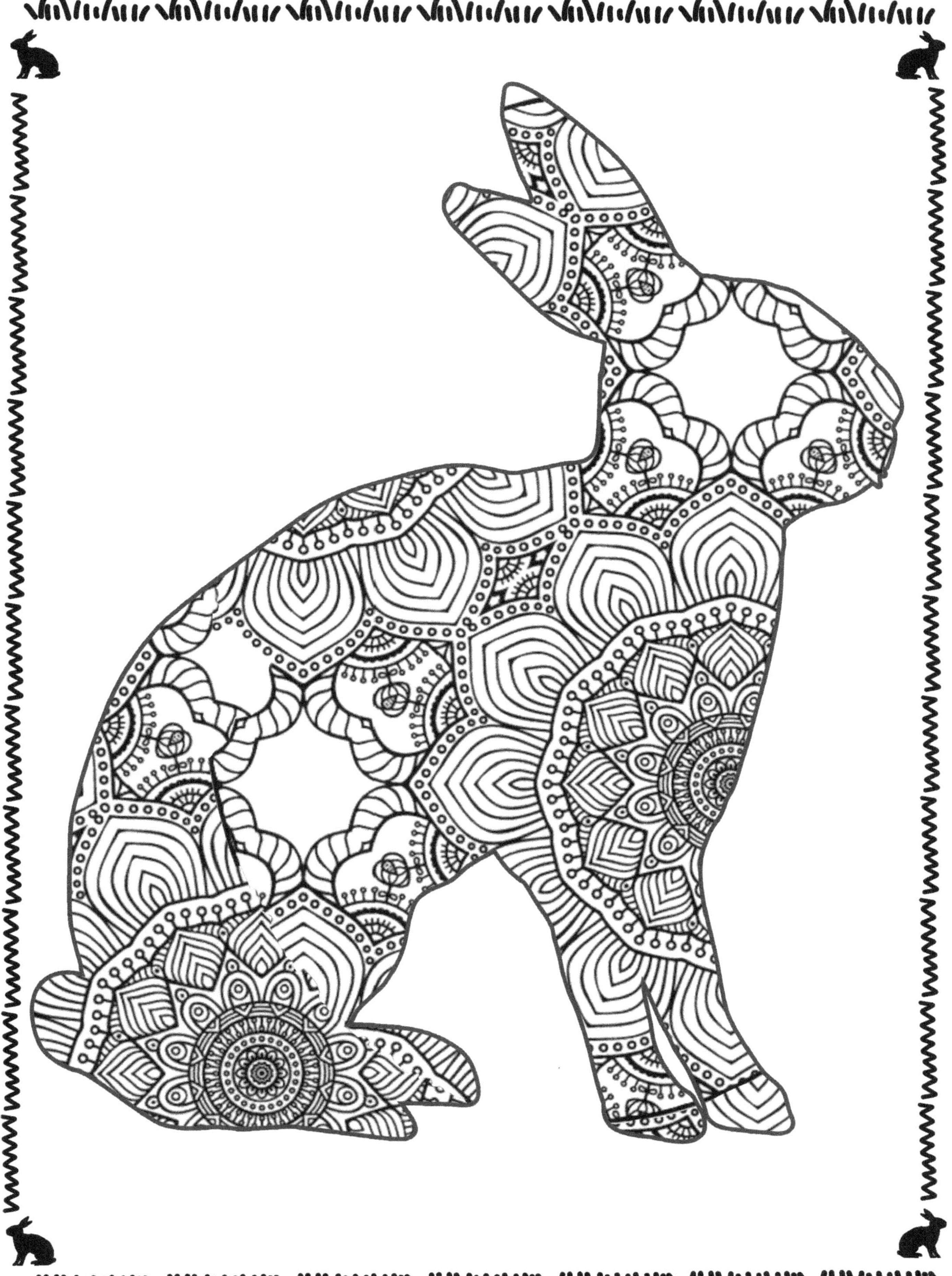

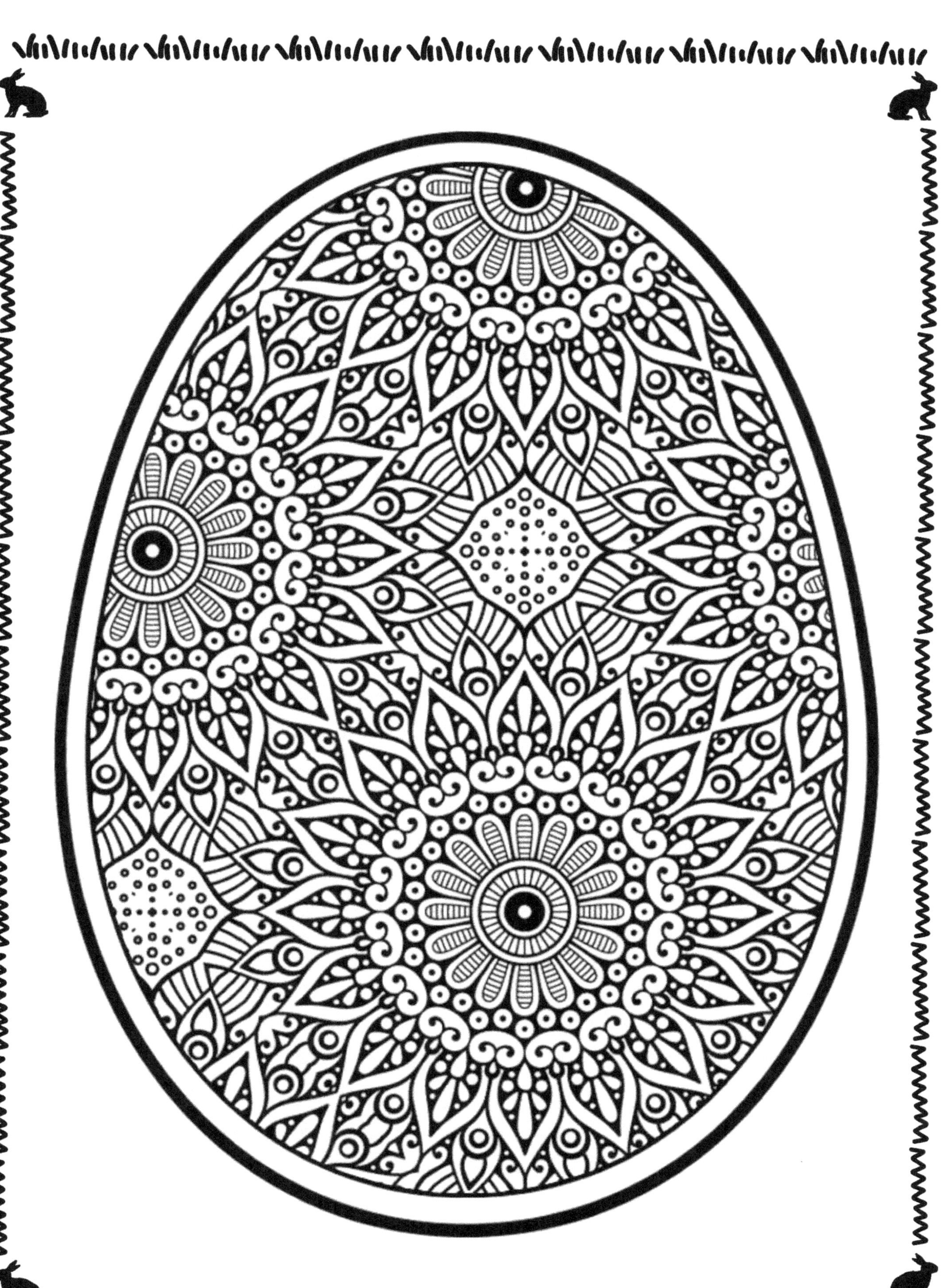

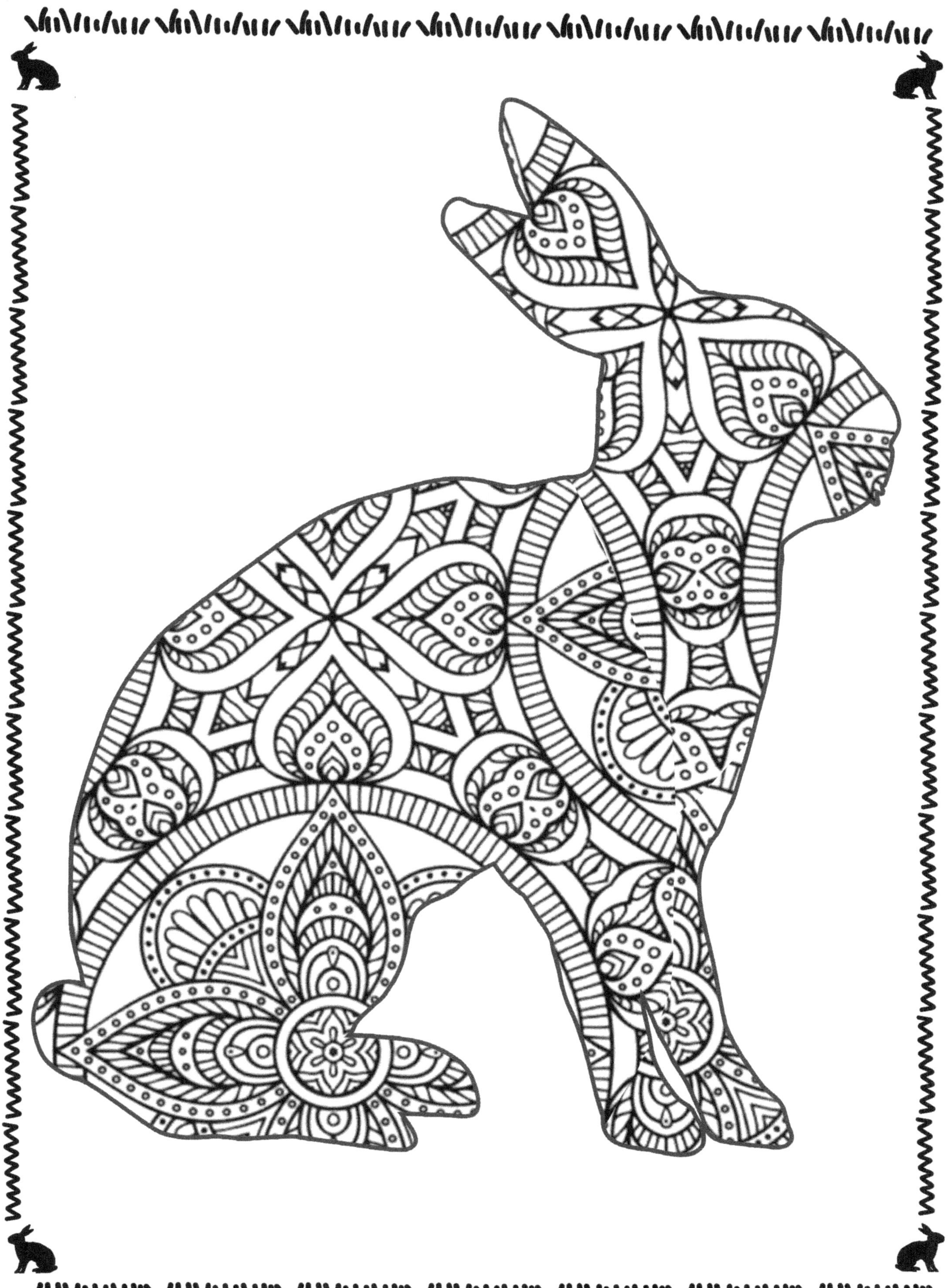

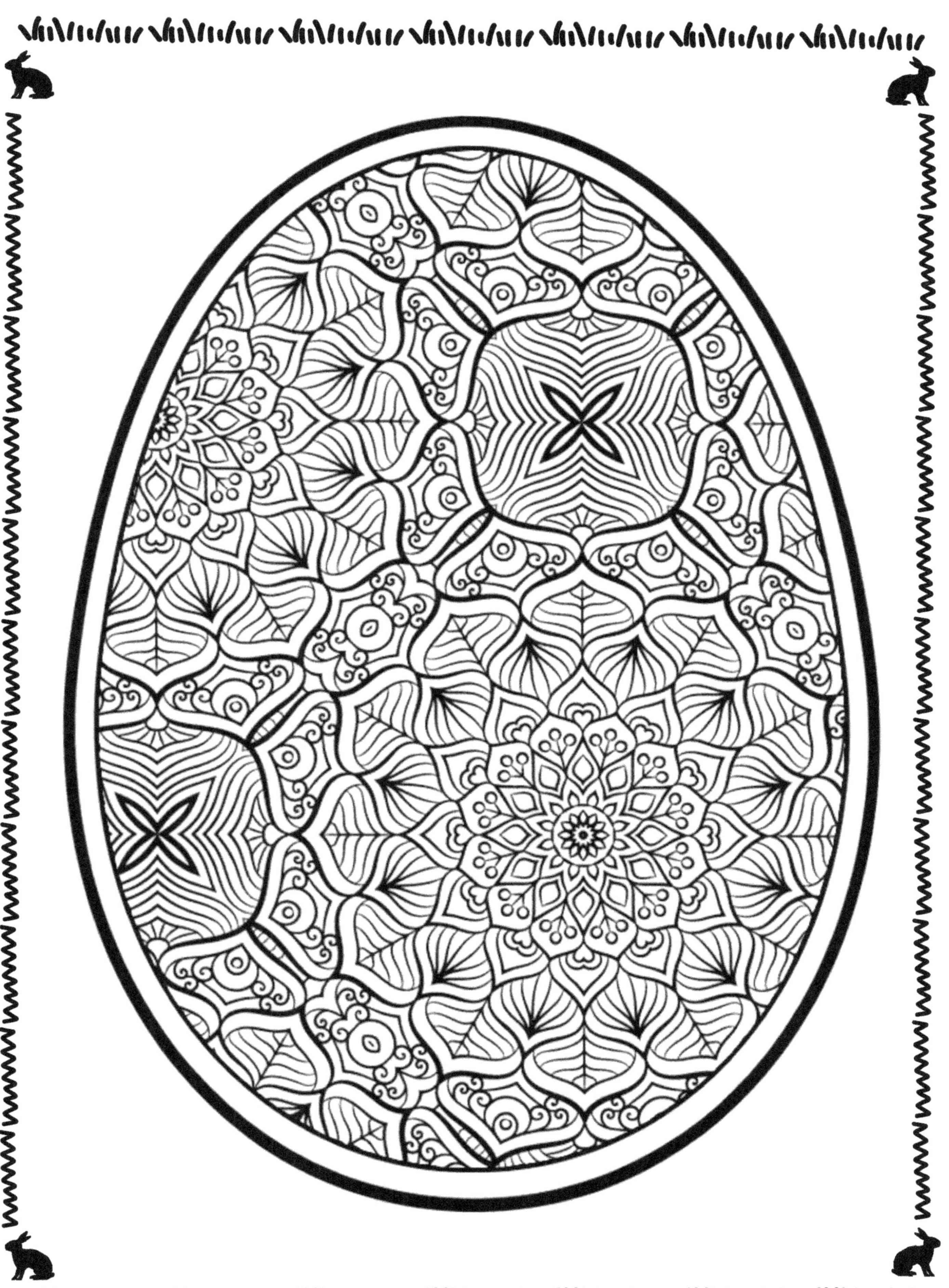

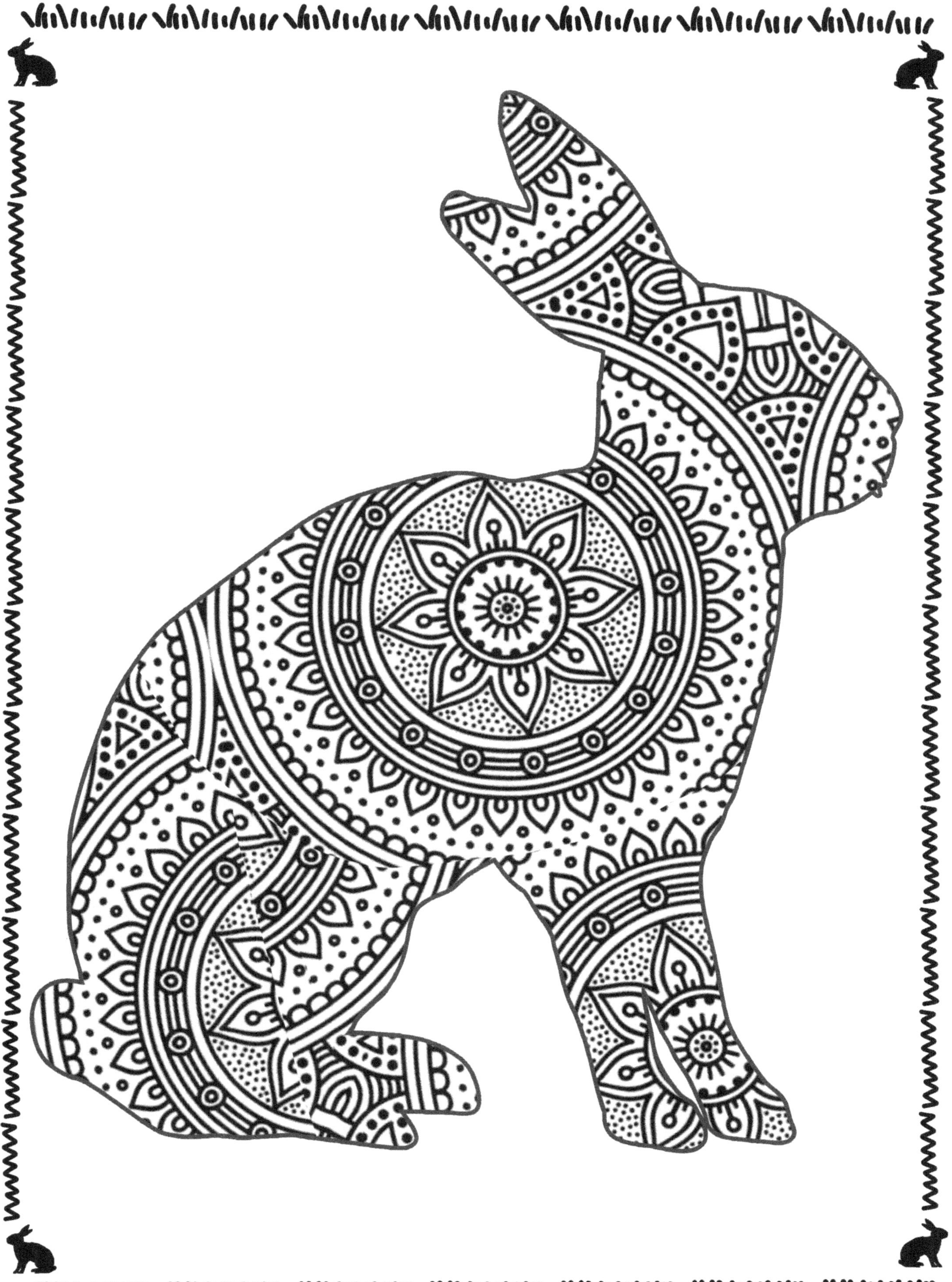

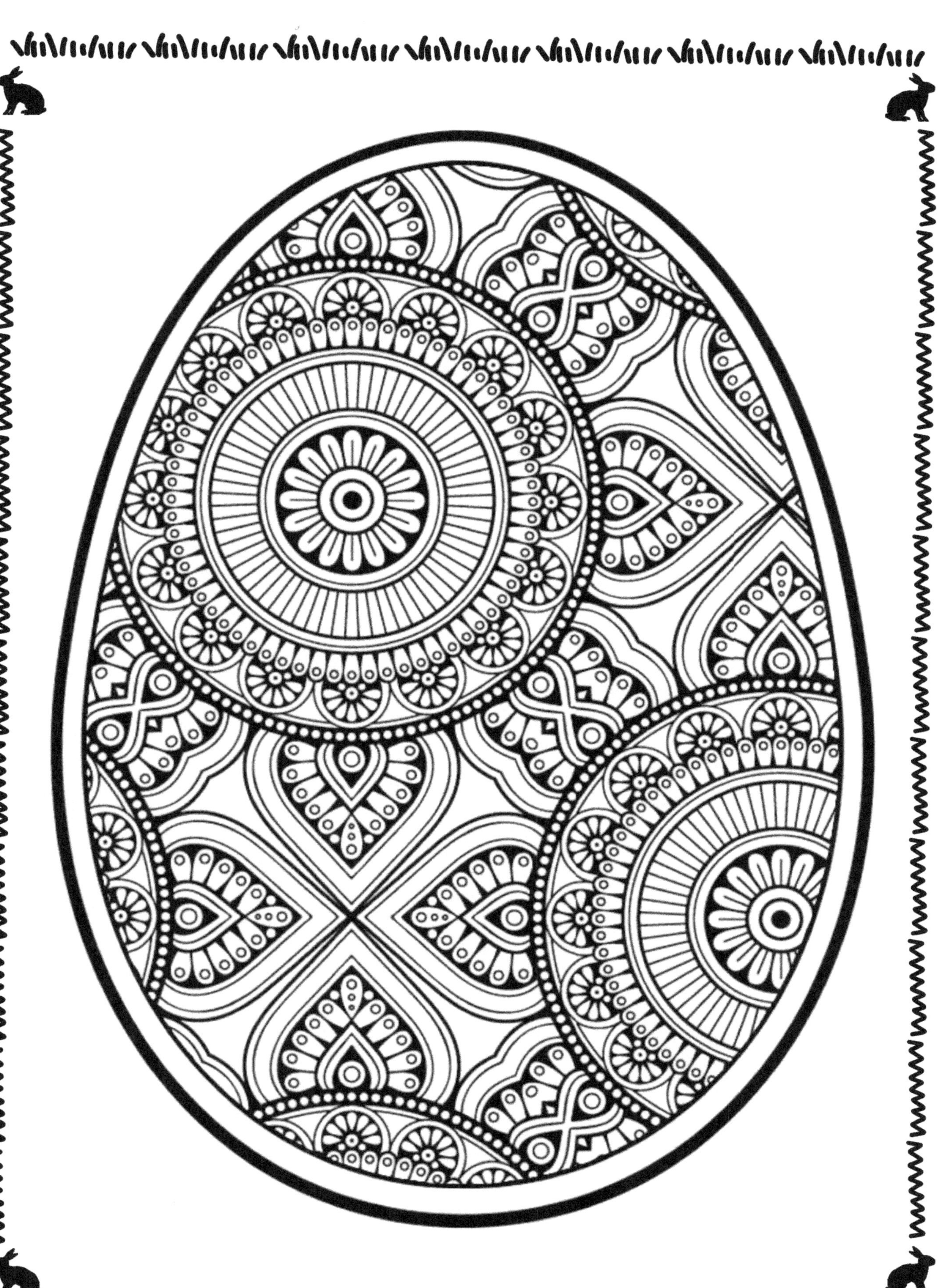

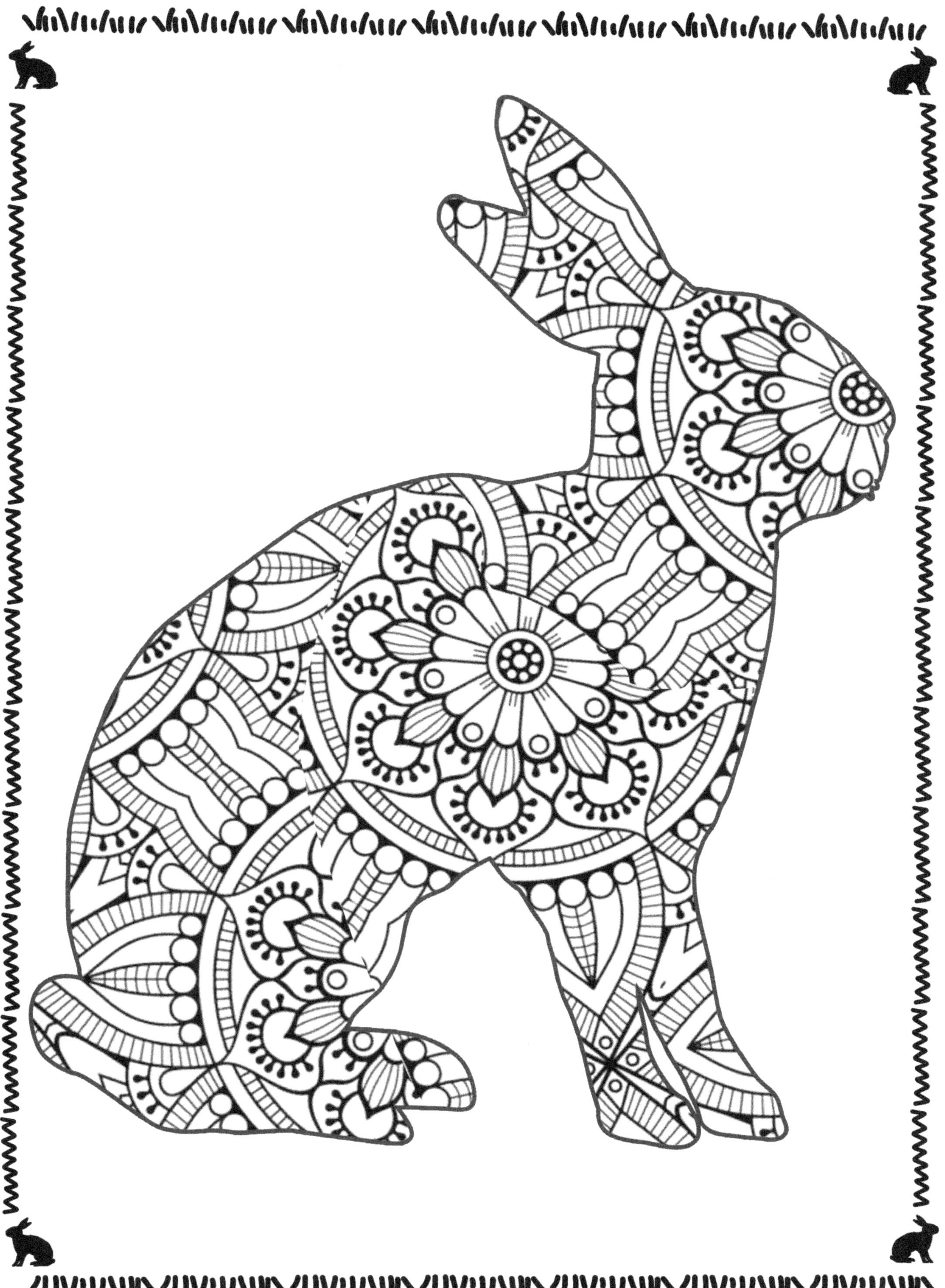

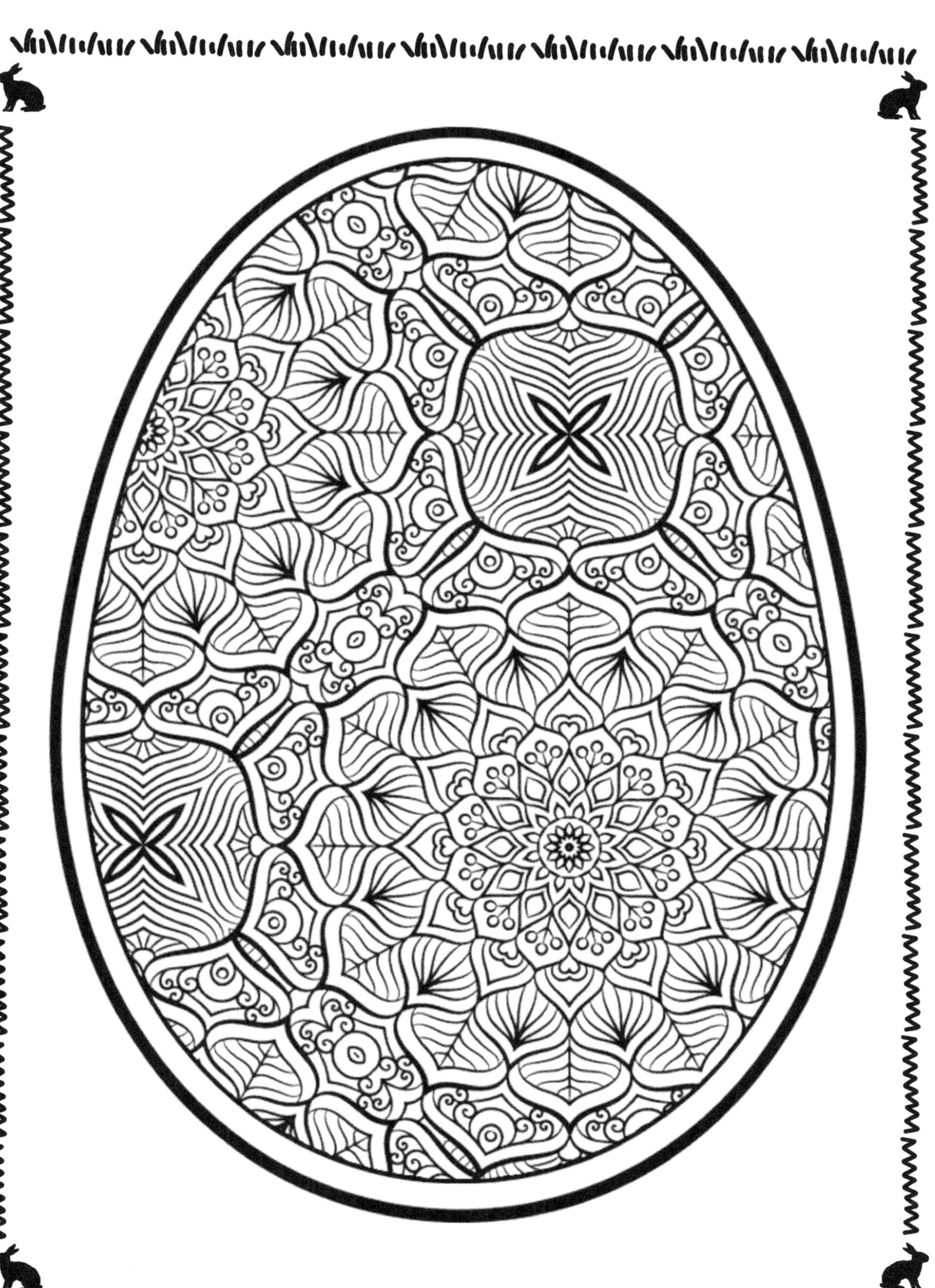

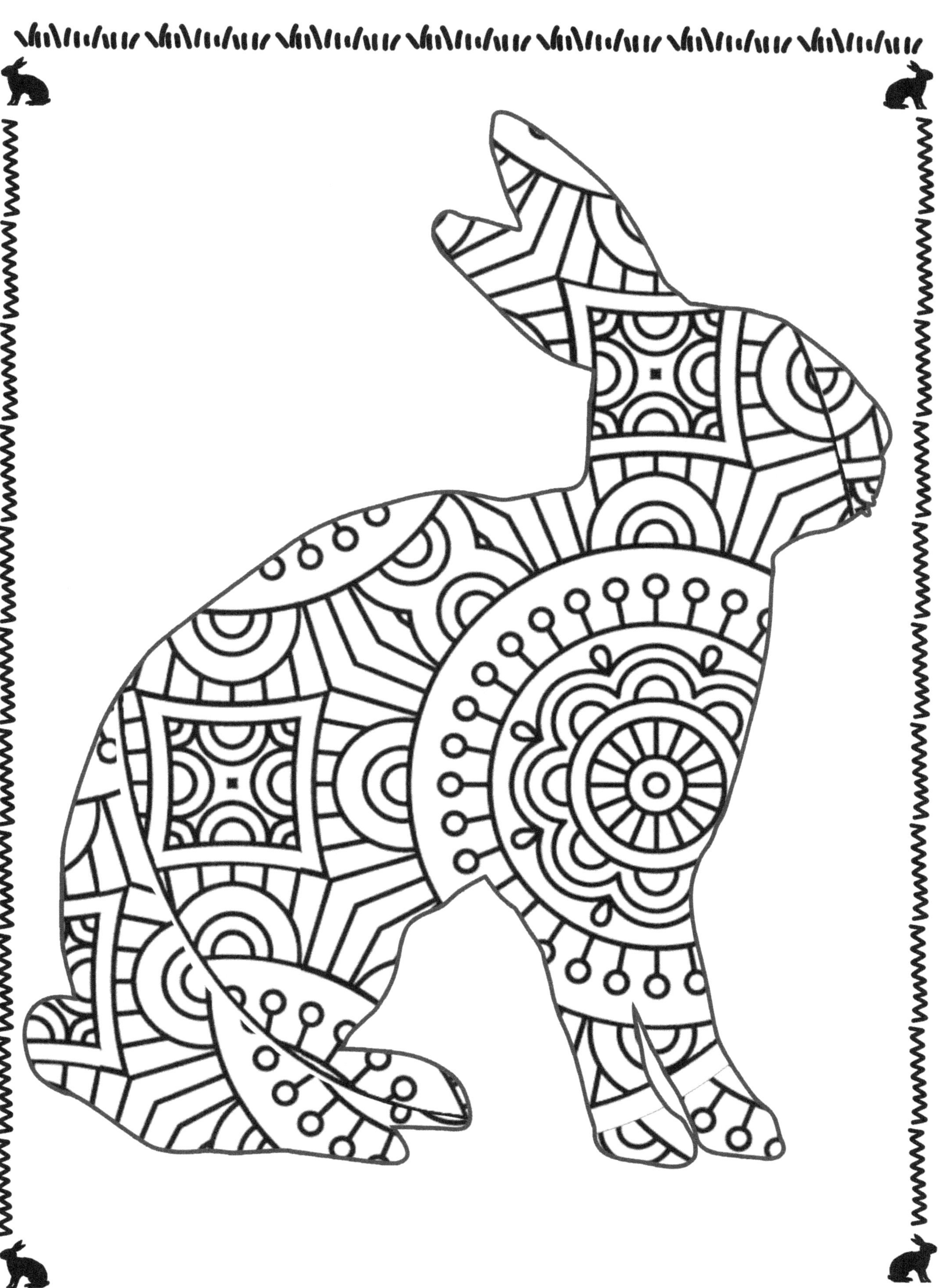

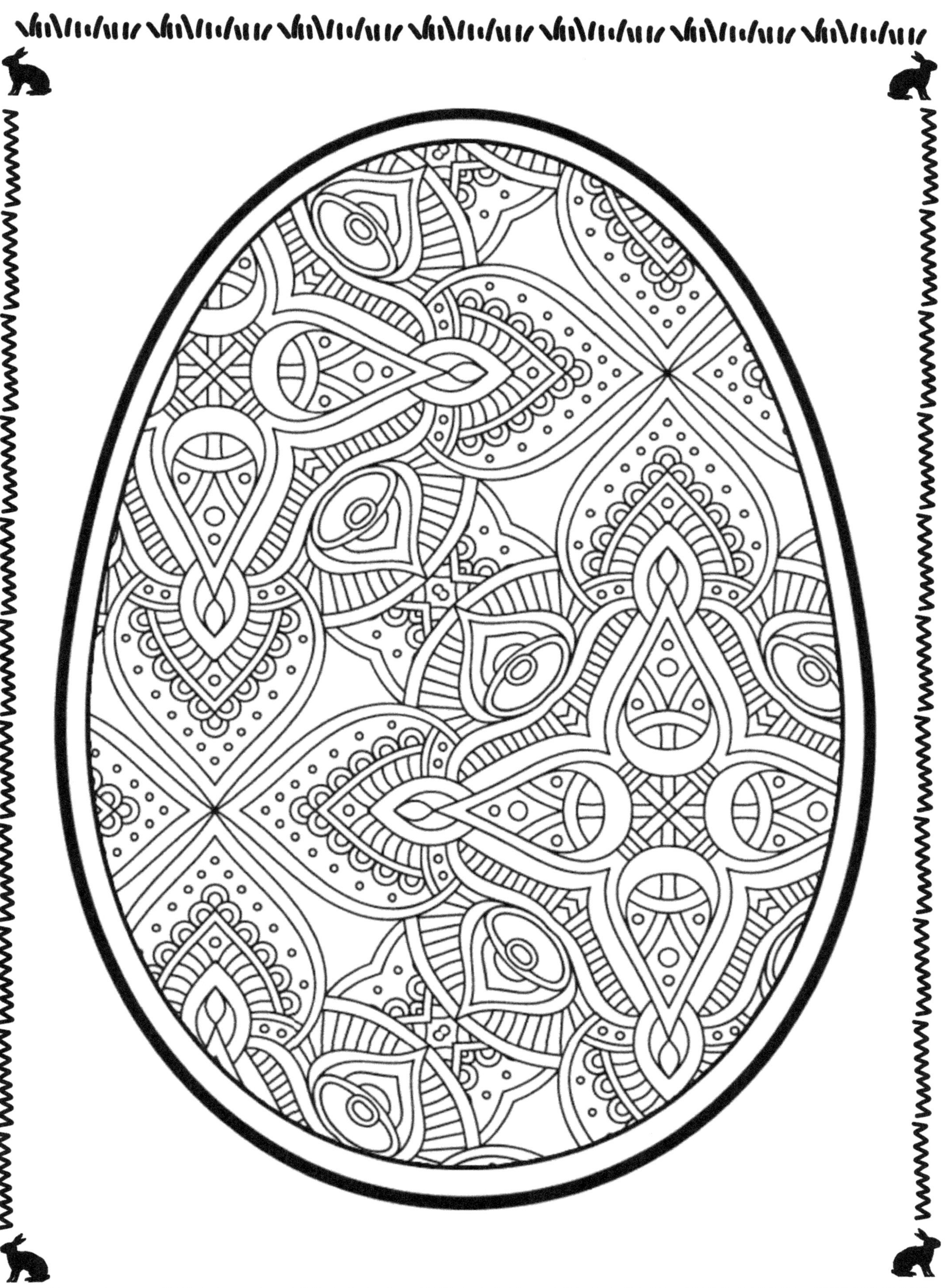

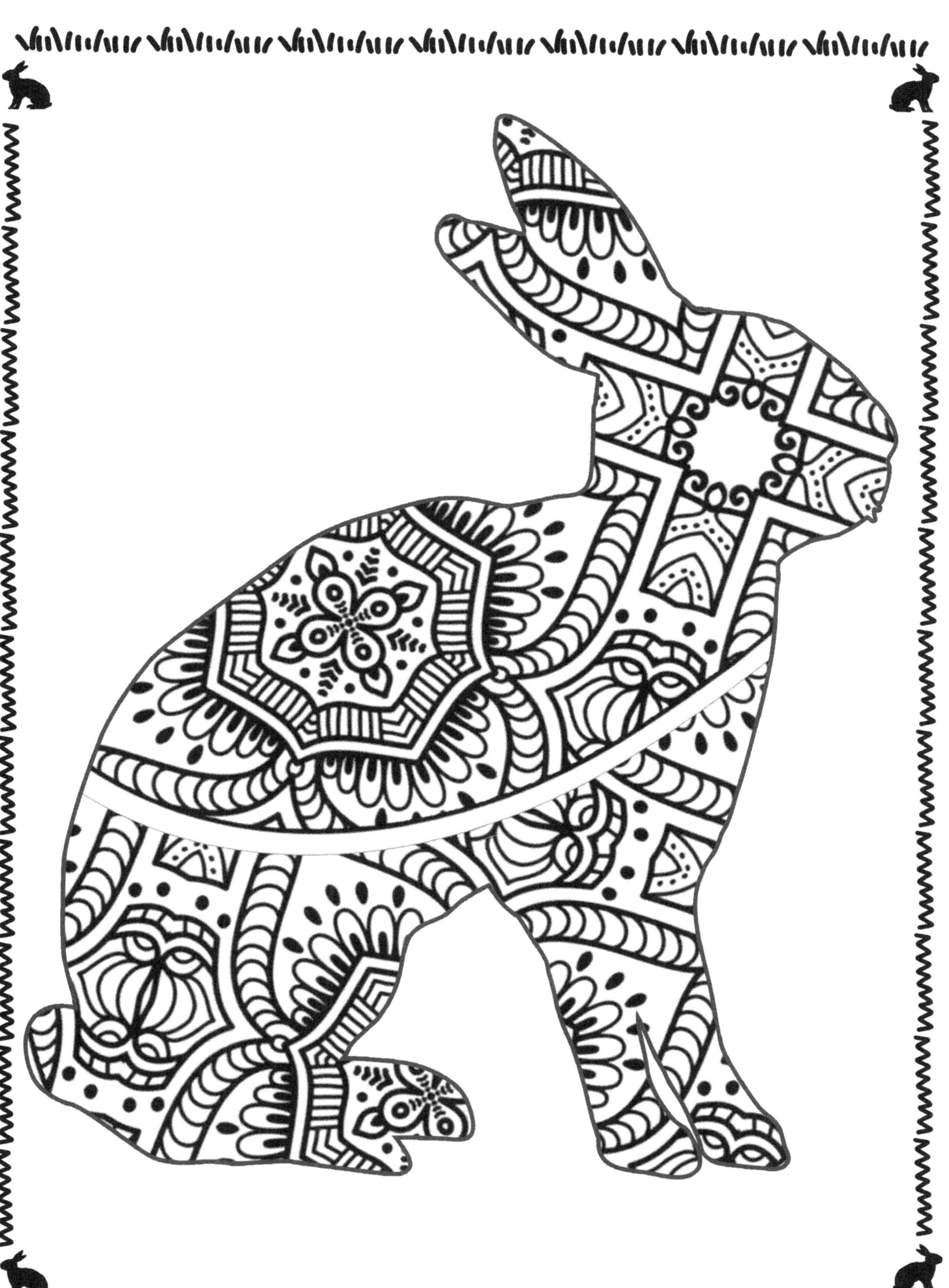

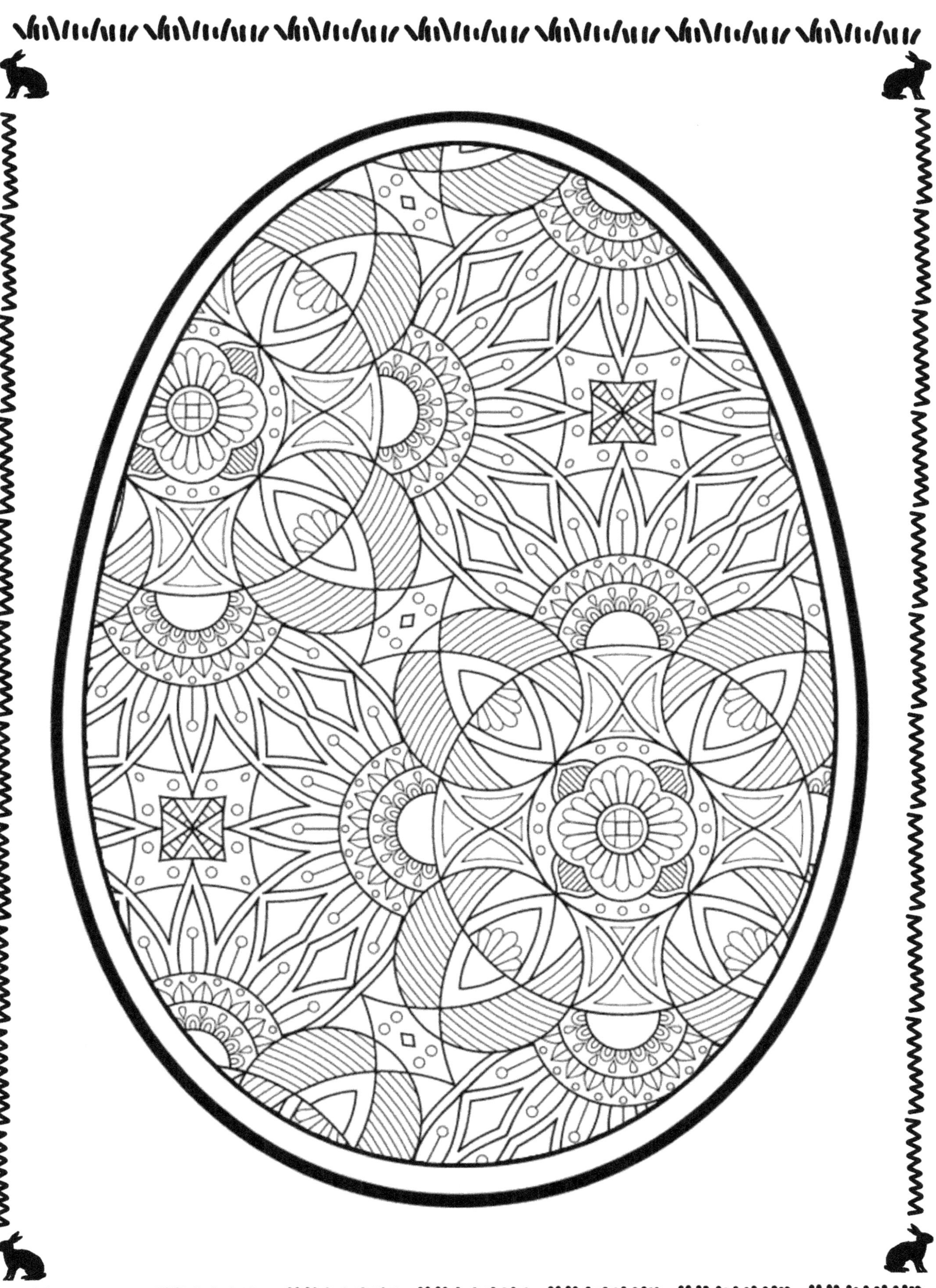

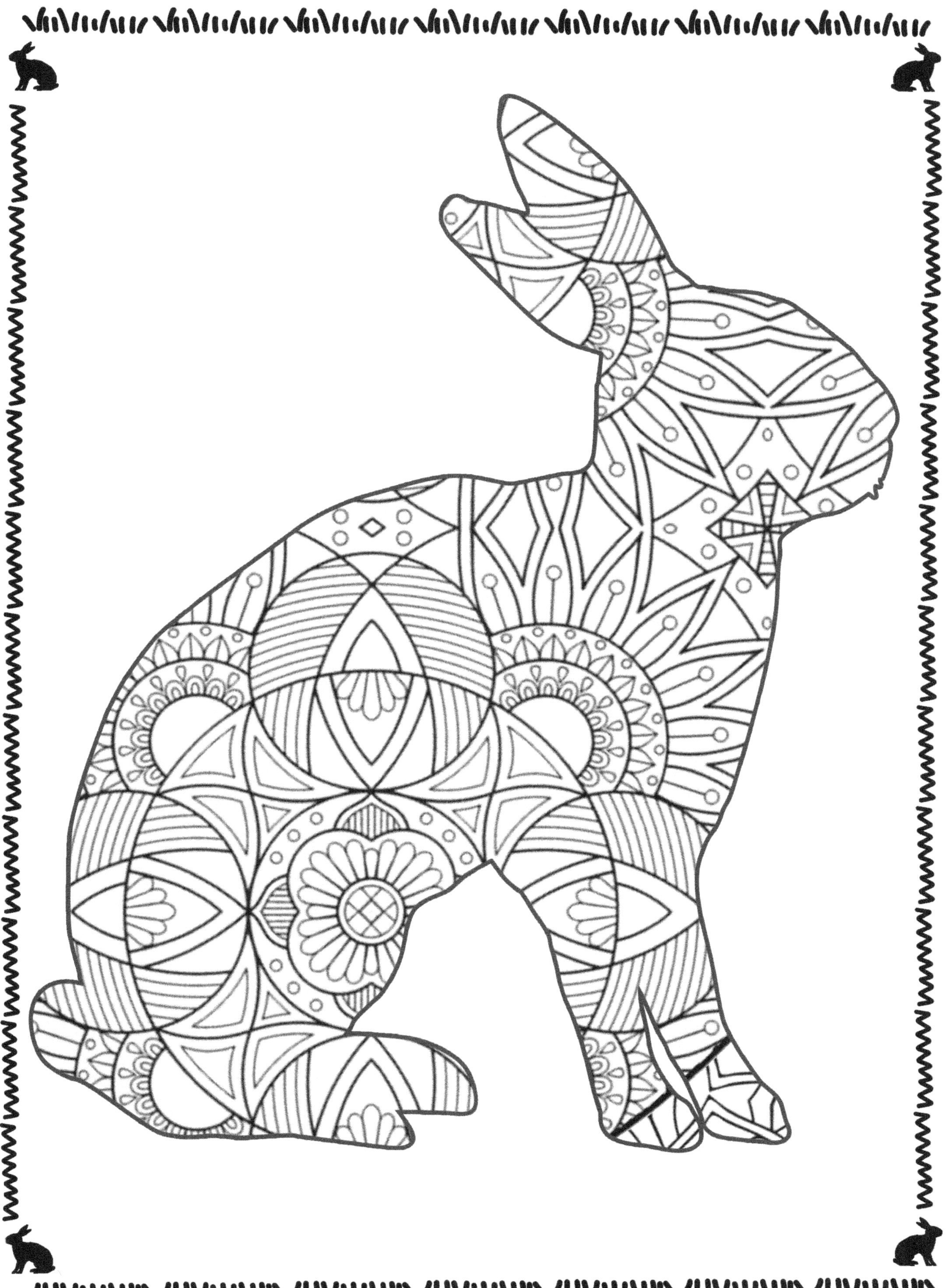

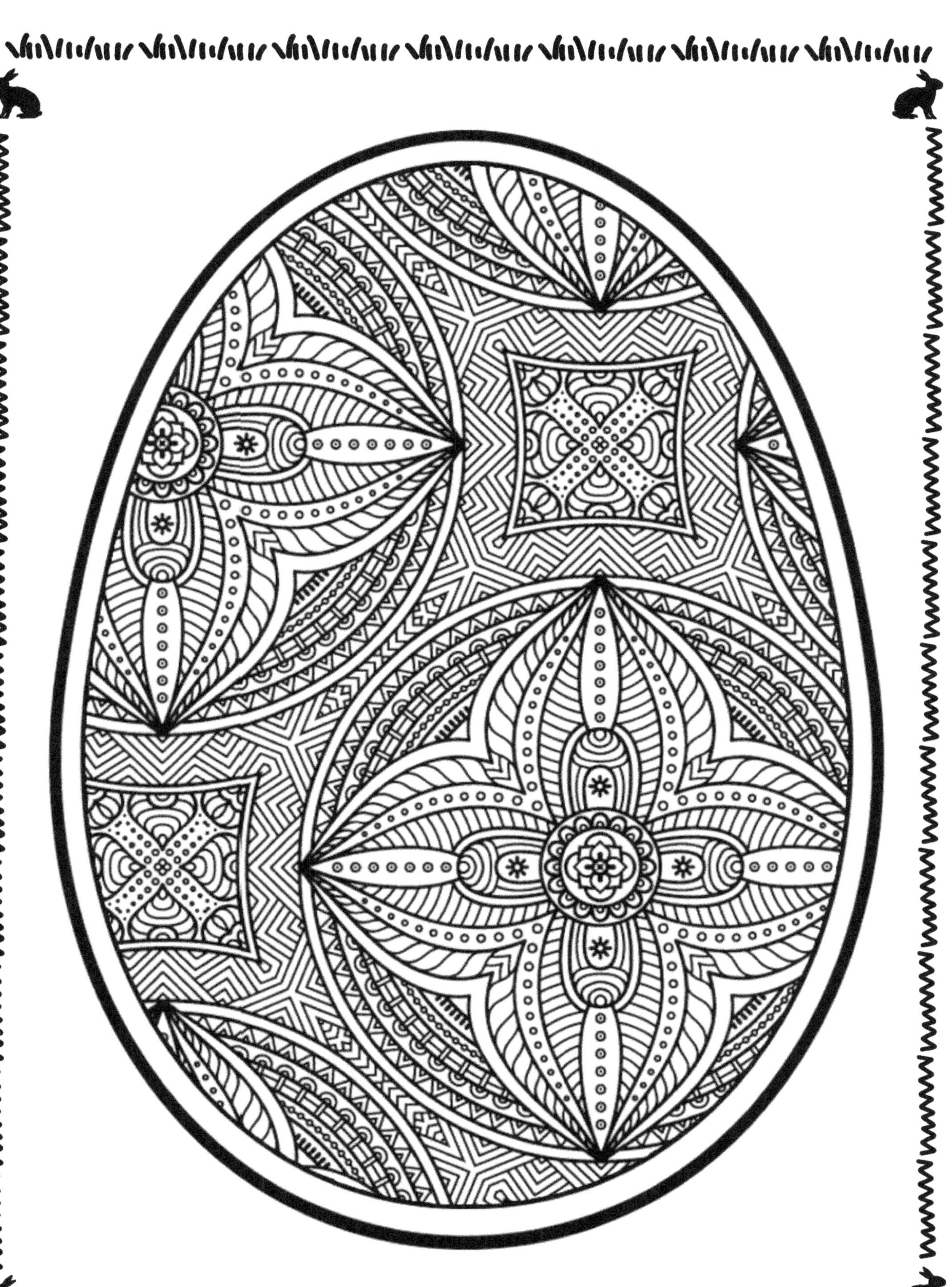

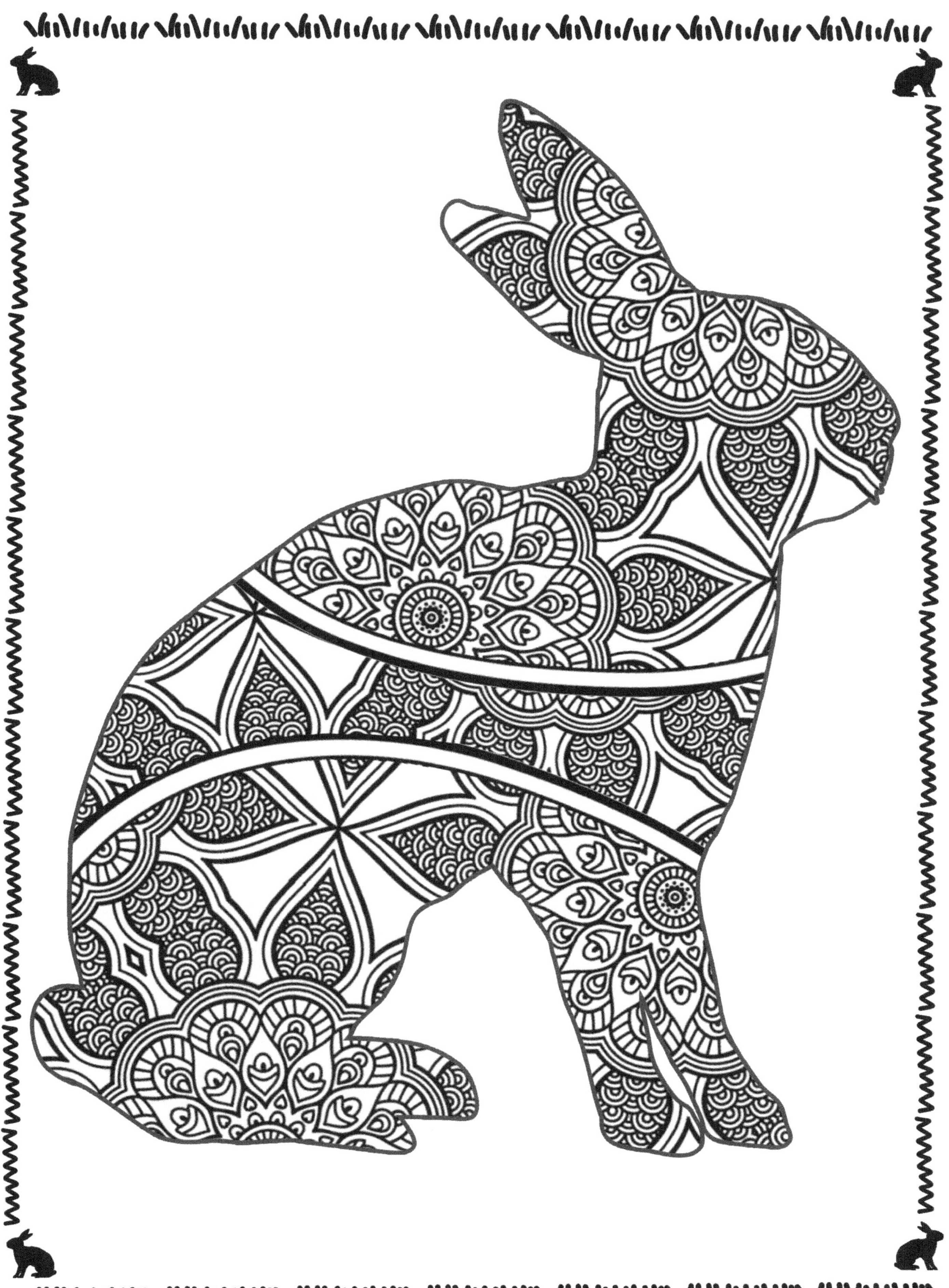

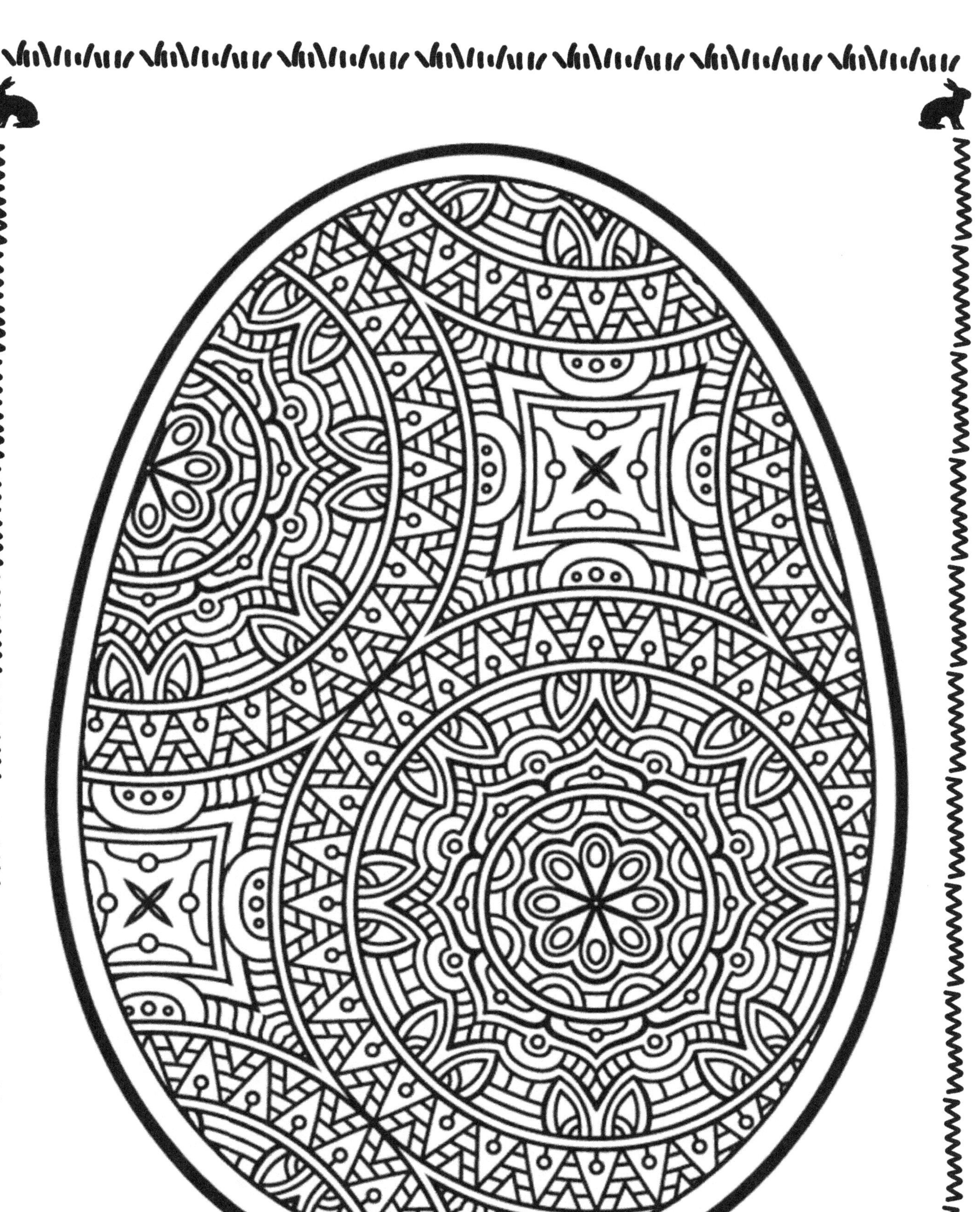

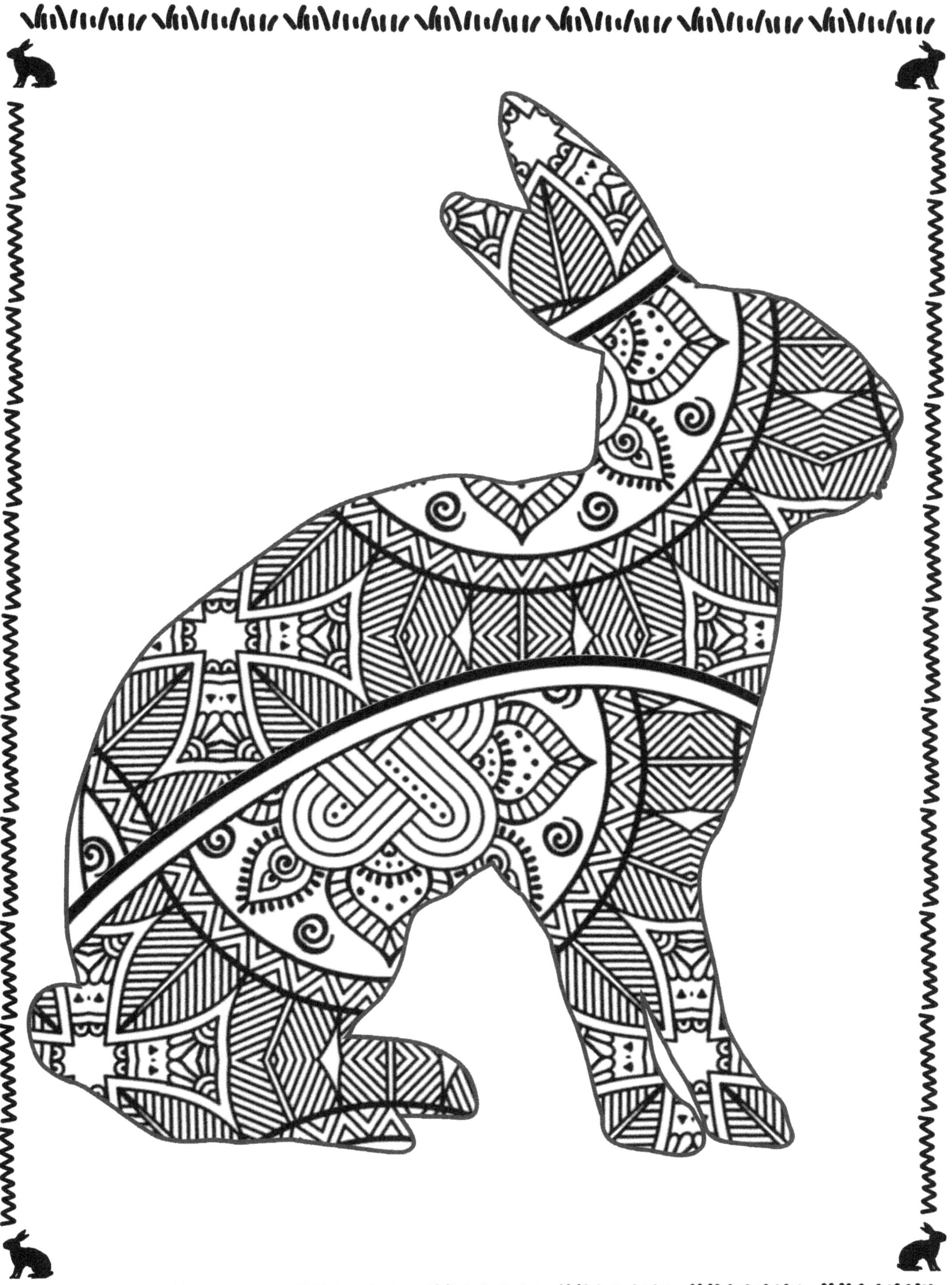

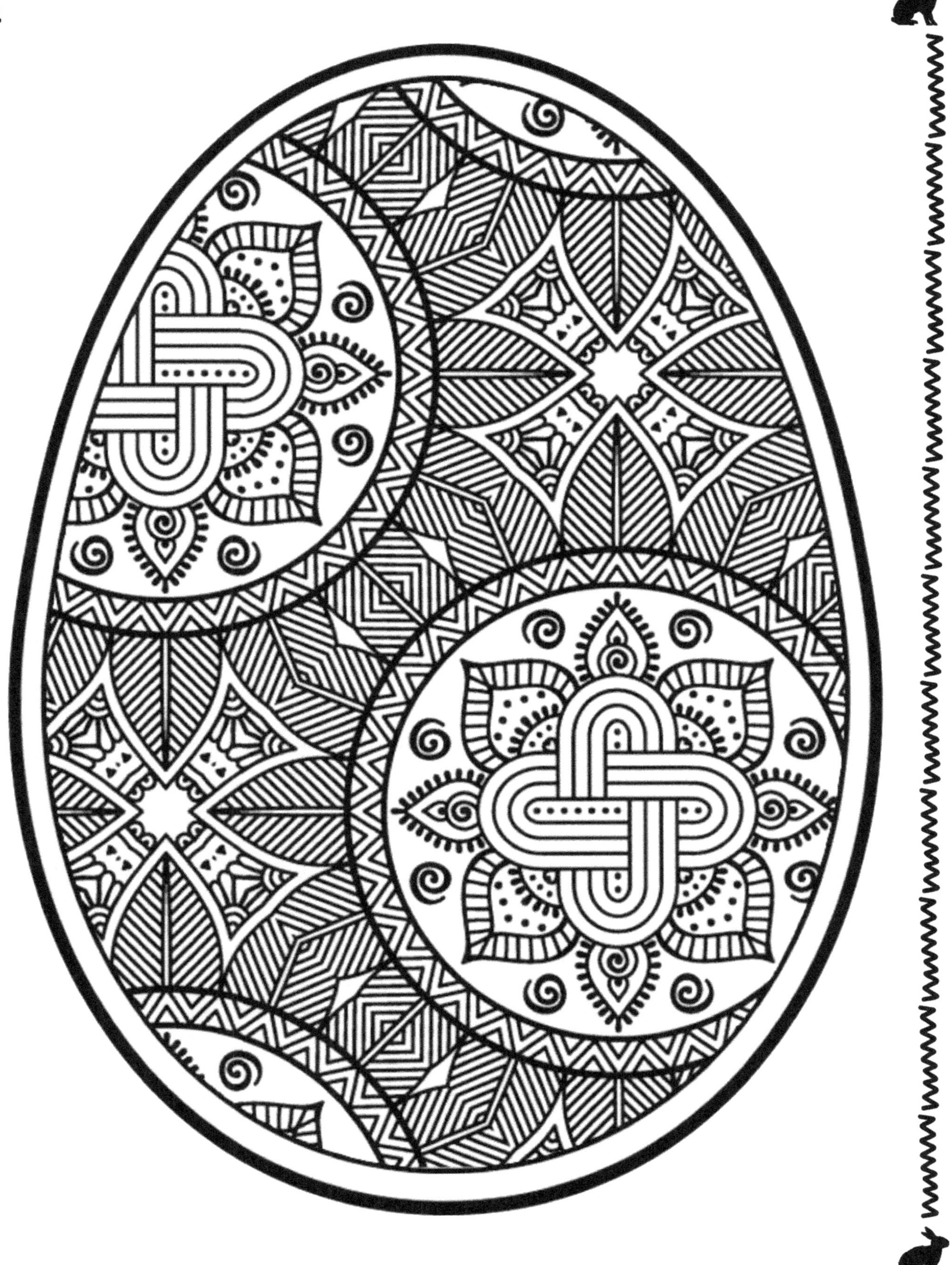

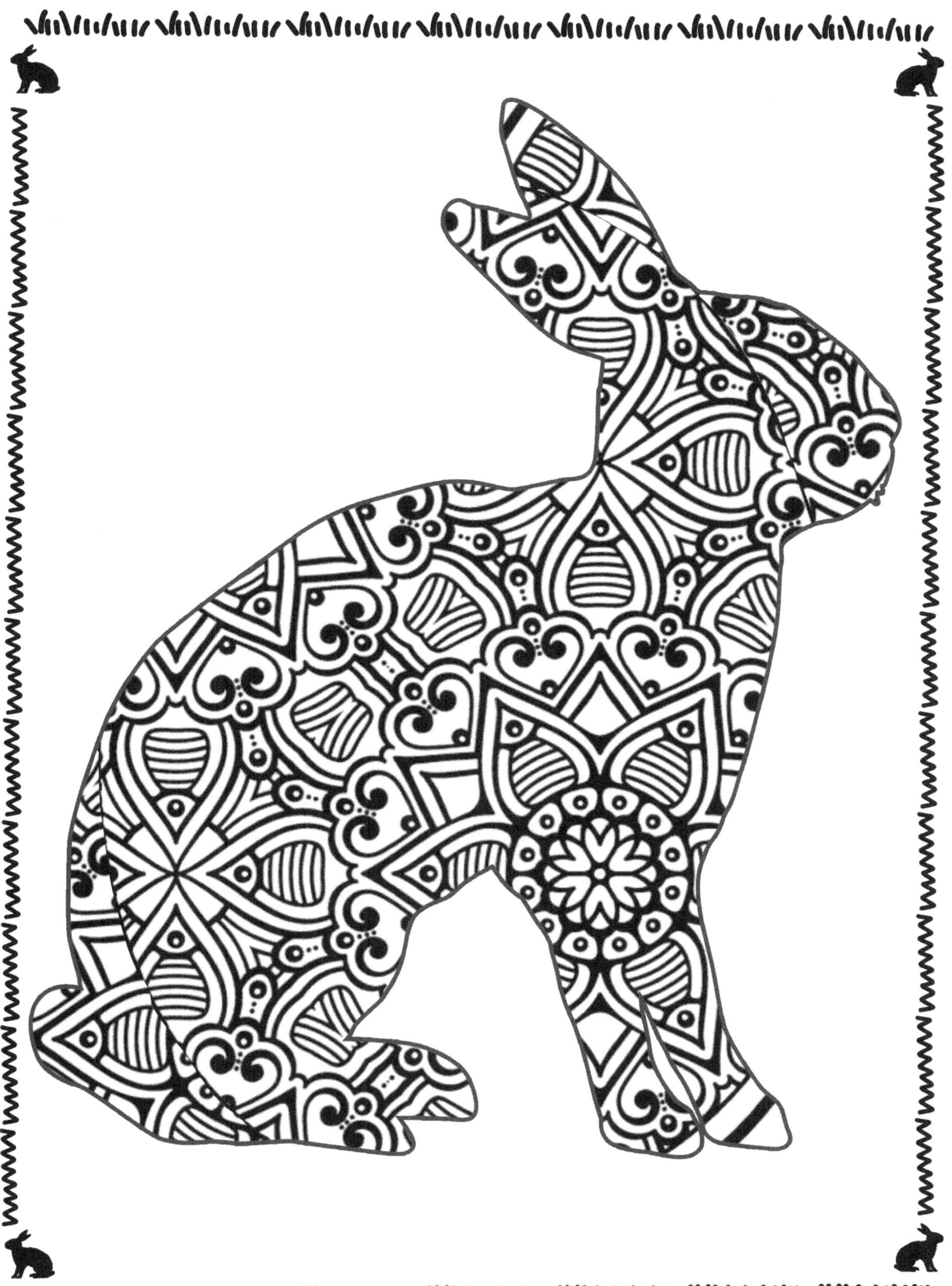

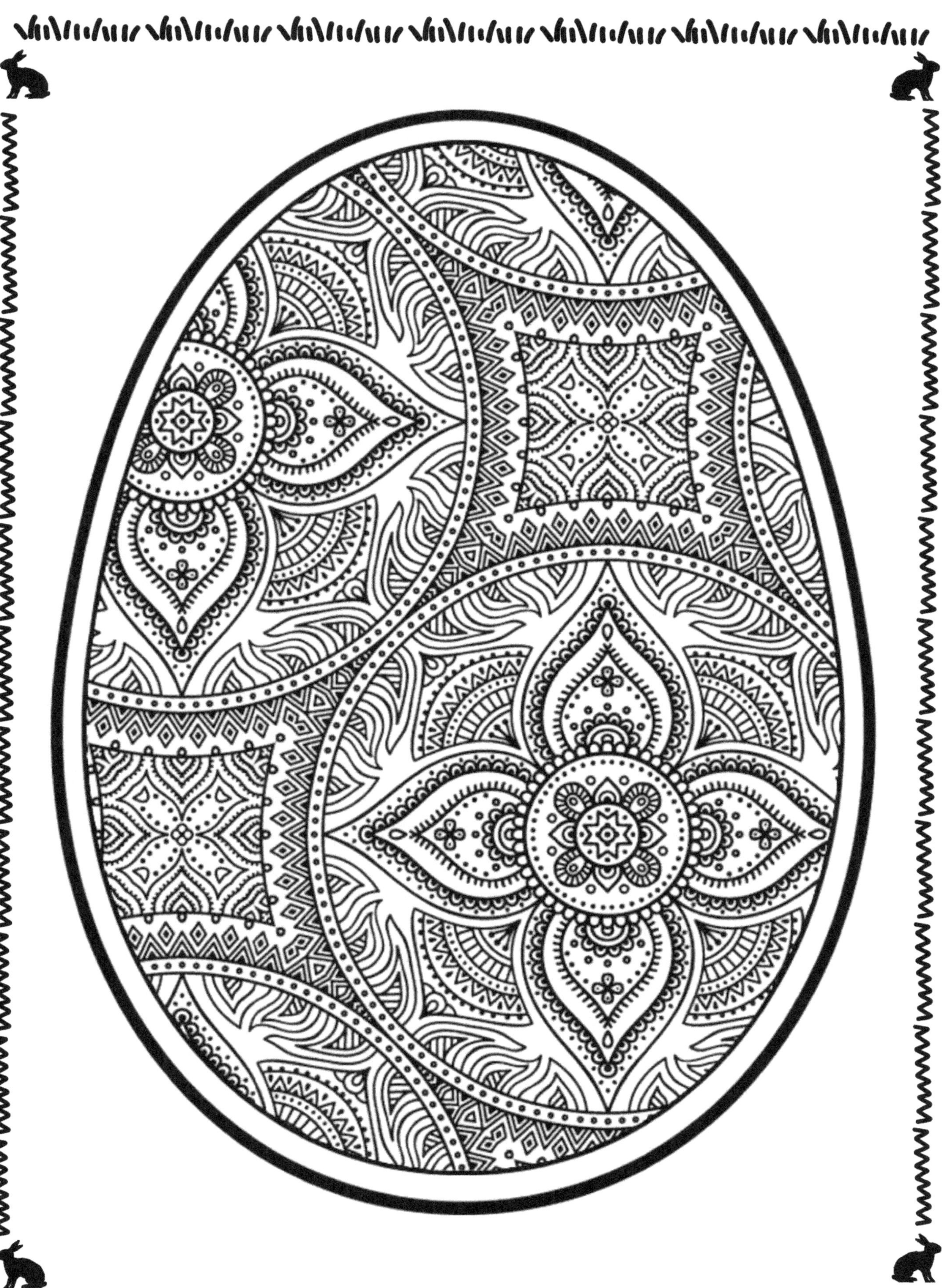

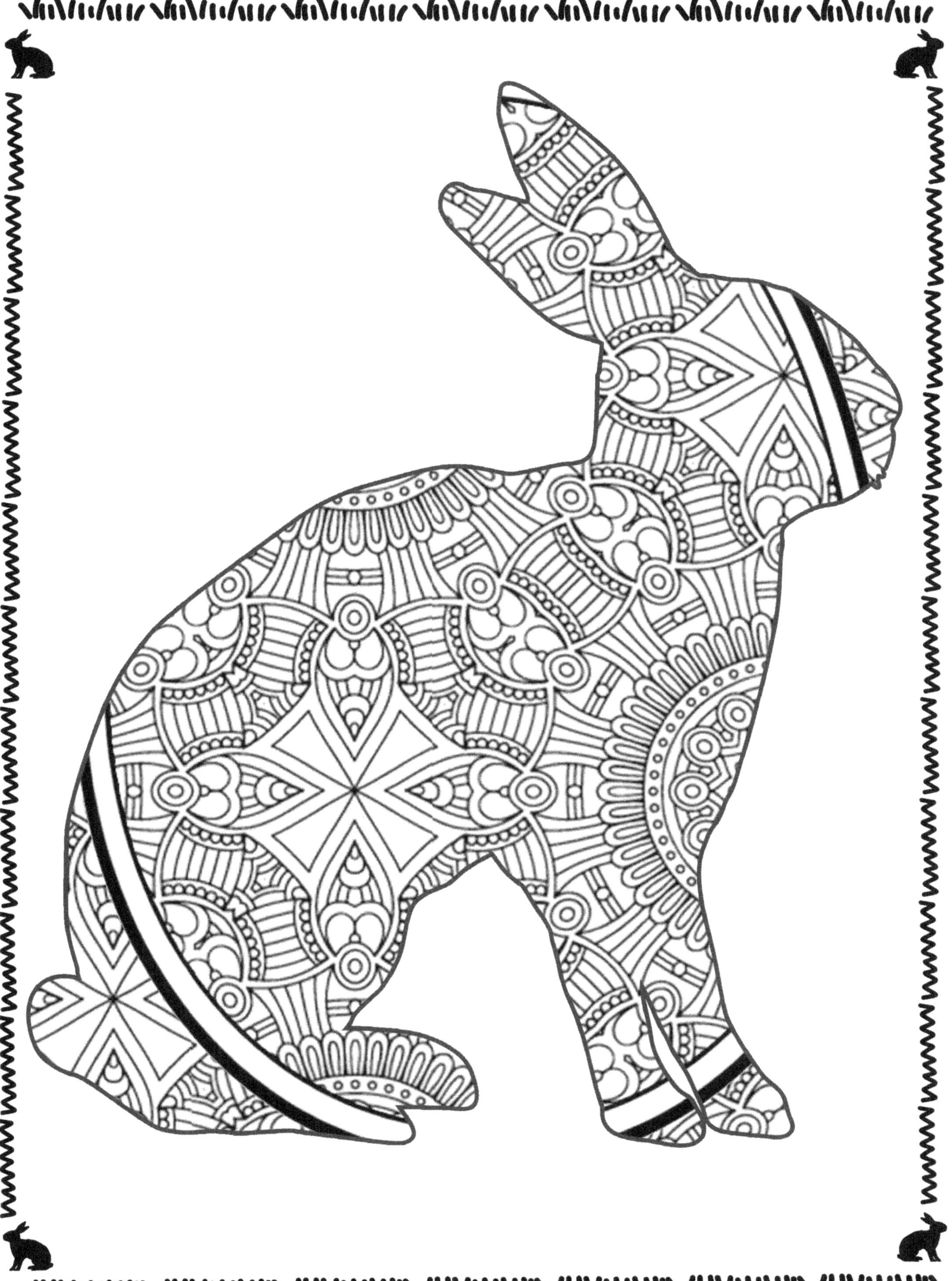

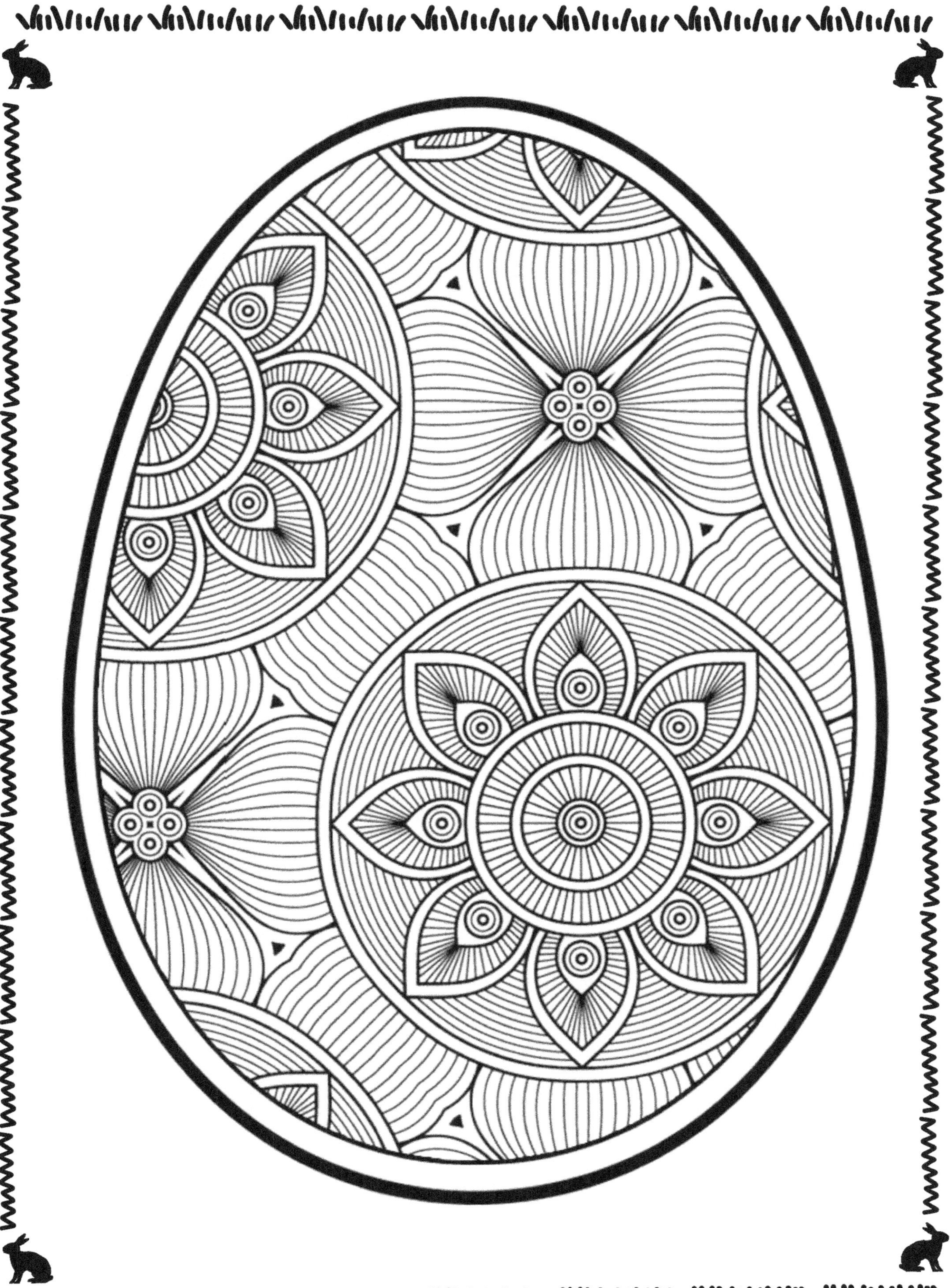